FROM
CV TO
SHORTLIST

FROM CV TO SHORTLIST

JOB HUNTING FOR PROFESSIONALS

TONY VICKERS

**KOGAN
PAGE**

YOURS TO HAVE AND TO HOLD

BUT NOT TO COPY

First published in 1997

Kogan Page Limited
120 Pentonville Road
London N1 9JN

© Tony Vickers

British Library Cataloguing in Publication Data
A CIP record for this book is available from the British Library.

ISBN 0 7494 1978 4

Typeset by BookEns Ltd, Royston, Herts.
Printed in England by Clays Ltd, St Ives plc

Contents

Acknowledgements

This book is not based on original work. Essentially, it is a synopsis which brings together the work of many scholars, practitioners and commentators. It presents a comprehensive overview of important issues now facing managers and professionals during their job hunting. As such, it is heavily dependent on a wide range of secondary sources, and I am therefore particularly indebted to a large number of earlier writers, not all of whom I have been able to acknowledge in this bibliography.

It is a pleasure to acknowledge the information, advice and help which I have received from so many talented people in Great Britain and the United States during the preparation of this book. They have influenced my thinking and I appreciate their guidance and support. I would like to thank all the senior managers and professionals whom I had the pleasure of advising and working with during my career with Coutts Consulting Group plc. I owe a special debt to my former Director colleague, Dennis Shadbolt, for his many creative ideas and support, and to Dr George Erdos of Newcastle University, both of whom provided the initial impetus for this book. I would also like to thank my former colleague, Dr Mike Smith of UMIST, for his valuable insights into psychometric testing. Several of my colleagues in the University of Salford willingly gave me their comments and suggestions and I would like to thank Professor Frank Neal, Rodger Adkins, Ian Hall, and Sandi Mann of the BNFL Corporate Communications Centre. I am particularly grateful to Joanna Wilson of the

University Library for her research assistance. My special thanks go to Dr Richard Macdonell for his continual encouragement and stimulating discussion. My MBA and MSc students deserve special mention for their helpful suggestions and feedback.

In the USA, several libraries helped me to locate modern research material; I would like to thank staff in Tulane University, Louisiana State University, the Universities of Mississippi and Alabama, and Professor Gibb Aiken of the University of Virginia for his findings on the changing nature of work. I am especially grateful to J P Warner of New England Insurance, Boston, for his generous hospitality and case study material and to the many business contacts who provided such informative conversation and ideas.

To my publisher, Philip Mudd, I owe a special debt of gratitude for accepting this book for publication, and to Susan Pollock, my Commissioning Editor, go my thanks for her patience and editing skills. As always, my main debts are personal ones. To Adrian and Hilary Vickers go my particular thanks for their valuable suggestions on earlier drafts. Last, but not least, my very special thanks to my wife Joan for her continued feedback, encouragement and support. Whatever faults remain are my own responsibility. I have enjoyed researching and writing this book and hope it will prove interesting, informative and useful.

Introduction

From CV to Shortlist is written specifically for managers and professionals. If you are an aspiring manager or professional, keen to make a success of your career, then three important issues will underpin your future development:

- You will need to actively manage your own personal effectiveness and become responsible for your own career and professional self-development.
- You will need to understand how the world of work is changing and its impact on organisations, careers and jobs.
- You will need to market yourself effectively, emphasising your continual employability by updating your skills and becoming adaptable and flexible.

Do not assume that by itself this book will find you the job, or occupation, or even career that you are looking for. Rather it will provide stimulation and give a sense of direction so that you become motivated to search more effectively. In the process we aim to give you a rich and accurate picture of what it takes to find jobs or work and to stay employable in a turbulent world.

Nevertheless, this book will go well beyond any preconceived notion that with an up-to-date CV, a covering letter, and a few contacts you will soon land the job you need. Things are no longer like that. Instead, we endeavour to show you how to become more innovative in your approach and how to display your skills and achievements. Surfing the Internet, cultivating your impression management, joining professional forums and improving your networking are just some of the approaches we discuss. We also help you to generate ideas and meet the challenge of finding a role which best suits your personality, talents and experience. To do this we will concentrate on the twin components of successful job hunting:

First, we will carefully examine the *content of your job hunting*. We will cover how you set your goals, design your marketing strategy, develop your CV and covering letters. In addition, we will show you how to research the labour market, network intelligently, use the Internet and succeed at interview.

Secondly, we will also explore the *context in which your job hunting is set*. We will analyse how changing environments affect careers and jobs as well as the workplace and the labour market. In additional we will explore how global initiatives, new organisational forms, and the rapid emergence of a knowledge-based information economy will influence your job hunting. In the last chapter we will look at ways to protect your future employability.

Our aim is to give this book a distinctive flavour and an innovative approach. Much of this stems from the emphasis we place on the need for you to integrate and harmonise the *content* and *context* of your job hunting. Think of these as being *symbiotically related*. In other words, both parts rely on each other so that they can continue to exist and develop. The success of your job hunting will largely depend on understanding how these two important issues relate to each other.

However, *From CV to Shortlist* is also designed to provide you with advice, information, support and ideas at whatever stage you have reached in your career. After professional training you may be planning your first move into management; you may be looking for your second or third career move; or you may be in line for a senior appointment. Again, you may feel you are reaching a plateau or want to know how to refresh a tired career. Alternatively, you may be seeking advice on a career change after downsizing or redundancy. As your family commitments alter, you may decide now would be a good time to re-enter the labour market.

Whatever your circumstances, this book endeavours to act

as your guide and tool-kit. It is a resource book to be consulted and used at different times and for different purposes. It emphasises various ways you can develop your preparedness and self-assurance. It is designed to enliven your job hunting to bring you closer to where you want to be and what you want to do. Overall, its style is practical, encouraging and linked to your future career development.

Job search, job hunting, work search, job finding: these are different terms which you are likely to use in varying contexts. In many respects they are similar, and in various parts of this book you will find they are interchanged. However, when it comes to career change, then we are experiencing something very different, as we shall discuss later on. Whatever you are faced with, job or career change, you are trying to tackle and solve what is essentially a complex problem. To approach it in a rational and constructive way, you will need to do two things:

1. Discover what pieces of information will be most useful to you in arriving at a solution.
2. Learn to put these pieces together in a logical pattern in order to solve the problem.

Already, there is strong evidence that job searching will become increasingly demanding and problematical in the future. Managers and professionals will need to be more innovative and creative in their self-marketing. Their networking and impression management skills will have to be well-honed. They will require greater awareness of the ways modern information technology can help in finding work which will be both satisfying and enriching. This is because of the strong movement on both sides of the Atlantic towards the development of a knowledge-based information economy. In the same way in which firms will use their 'knowledge base' to dominate labour markets, as a manager or professional you will need to ask yourself how you can continually update your skills and competencies to remain employable as a knowledge worker.

You may reflect that in your job hunting you are entering a

highly competitive and challenging world, where others may have far more to offer in terms of skills and experience. Yet it is invariably through your self-marketing and impression management skills that you will be successful. Part of the raison d'être of this book is to make your search for work exciting, challenging and interesting. View it as a well-crafted project which not only helps you to learn and be rewarded, but also provides a sense of achievement and personal satisfaction. *Do not look upon it simply as a one-off exercise.* Instead, you should consider your job hunting as:

- an integral part of your repertoire of essential skills which you use and polish during most of your career;
- a vital aspect of your personal investment portfolio, to be reviewed and revised as the market changes.

Let us now go forward to Chapter One. Here we will explore some of the important issues which make up the *context* in which your job hunting strategy is set. We will also show how these affect the way you operate and influence how successful you will be in achieving your objectives.

Part One:

Evaluating Change in the World of Work

1

Searching for Work in Turbulent Times: Changing Jobs and Careers

WHAT'S HAPPENING TO CAREERS?

Up to the early 1980s, many managers and professionals viewed their careers as orderly and predictable. The game plan was to climb a corporate hierarchy, while gathering knowledge, skills and experience on the way. By so doing you hopefully enhanced your position, status, prestige and rewards. During your twenties you would go through the exploratory stage of considering a range of options open to you. In your thirties you would focus on building your career on solid foundations. In your forties you would evaluate and review your progress. Your career was essentially linear and largely dependent on the traditional large, mechanistic, pyramid-shaped bureaucratic organisation. Like many professionals, you saw it as a succession of related jobs through which you moved in an ordered sequence. As you travelled the career path, often designed by the organisation, you built your reputation and skills. You also hoped your career would bring some of the benefits of challenge, autonomy and job satisfaction which managers and professionals were traditionally seen to enjoy. Even so, their actual experience may have been otherwise.

In addition you may have tried to progress faster than your colleagues through what is called *an internal labour market*, with its ladders and promotions, transfers and upgrades, demotions and departures. In it you saw people moving in, moving out, moving up or down. Within the market were well established selection and reporting procedures, job descriptions, compensation packages, performance evaluation and above all a political network, which you ignored at your peril.

Your career success was therefore clearly linked to the structure and size of the organisation. You could view and evaluate your career in two ways.

1. *Objectively*, in terms of how far and how quickly you had climbed, your level of responsibility at a particular age, your rewards package and your importance and power in the organisation.
2. *Subjectively*, in terms of how you felt about your job — was it interesting and rewarding, did it provide satisfaction and challenge, did you feel you were successful and fulfilled or simply stressed and frustrated.

However, since the early 1980s this traditional *dependent* view of managerial and professional careers has undergone a major evaluation. Dependency on the organisational career in the form of the corporate climbing frame has been severely affected by a combination of factors:

■ restructuring and downsizing, leading to leaner, flatter, decentralised organisations;
■ technological change, leading to delayering, networking, outsourcing and contingent workforces;
■ mergers, acquisitions, take-overs, joint ventures, leading to different strategies and staffing needs;
■ global competition and changes in the business climate, leading to cost-cutting and retrenchment.

In many respects, these changes are not continuous but discontinuous. Their combined effect can be likened to a tidal wave on managerial and professional careers. In its wake has come a series of important developments which are set out below:

- in order to survive organisations now have to respond much faster to changes in markets and technologies;
- increased workloads, larger spans of control and earlier responsibilities are the norm;
- greater emphasis on subcontracting, collaborative partnerships, core/peripheral workers;
- IT developments cause traditional middle manager roles to disappear;
- the boundaries and populations of organisations are much more fluid and dynamic.

As an exercise, collect examples of these from your work, from journals and newspapers or in discussion with your colleagues. Then consider in what ways they may affect your career, as well as your job hunting strategy, over the next few years.

Recent evidence suggests that less than 30 per cent of managers and professionals continue to pursue a traditional *organisation-dependent career path*. In terms of company tenure, whereas some 40 per cent of managers in 1975 had at least six years, by 1995 this had fallen to 16 per cent (source: *Bulletpoint* 34/96). In other words, a large majority now find themselves effectively de-coupled from the organisation and personally responsible for their own career and self-development. These are the new and rapidly expanding breed of independents who are not just building their own businesses. They also view their careers differently.

1. As a *set of different work experiences* gained over a period of time, what was the nature of the experience, what was learned, and how far is it transferable and marketable to others?
2. As a *store of knowledge and skills*, what are you able to offer to fit the work needs and culture of an organisation and how far will these confer a competitive advantage?

Instead of being linear, orderly and predictable, the independent career is already very different. Moreover, it is set to change even more in the next decade. Its direction will move from performing jobs to undertaking a series of work assignments. These become important because of the learning opportunities they provide. This partially explains the emphasis now made on work search rather than just job hunting. As a manager or professional you are far less likely to find your career embedded in a single firm in which hierarchy, procedures, longevity and seniority are considered important. Increasingly, independent careers will be based on projects, fixed term contracts, and job hopping rather than hierarchy climbing. Commitment to a particular role is likely to override your loyalty to a particular organisation. Career structures will become more short-term, less tidy and more diverse. They will be built from the resources within each individual. You will be valued and rewarded by those who take you on board because of your adaptability, tolerance of ambiguity and, hopefully, your portfolio of entrepreneurial and interpersonal skills. Therefore, as selectors become much more stringent in their requirements, you will find it even more crucial to market yourself well.

For the independent careerist, the emphasis will move from career development, which is essentially what organisations do to help you, to individual career planning, which is what you do to help yourself. Look upon your personal career plan as a road map of options and decision points involving a range of issues with which you will need to come to terms. These are outlined below.

Coming to terms with key issues in your personal career plan

1. How will you take charge of your career and in what ways will you develop it in the future?
2. Will your current qualifications, knowledge and experience keep you employable?
3. Is your personal skills inventory sufficiently transferable to add value to an organisation?
4. Do you have the energy and commitment to engage in lifelong learning?

Making sense of changing career landscapes, while at the same time managing your own development, will clearly require effort, motivation, single-mindedness and self-assurance. As the going becomes tougher so the rules have changed. It will be up to you to respond to the realities of a very different labour market. The watchword for all managers and professionals will be *'your career? – It's up to you'*. Do not look upon your managerial career as continuing to be serviced, maintained, developed and supported within a paternalistic organisation. Instead, the new environment of the independent careerist will place a heavy emphasis on you as an individual managing and promoting your own career assets.

Here are a number of tips to enable you to do this.

■ *Tip 1* – Treat your career as your greatest asset. First, look closely at the general abilities you possess to perform well in most jobs; your level of intelligence; your creativity and innovation; your drive, energy and motivation; your educational attainment and the level and quality of your credentials. Ask yourself if these are sufficient; if they need to be improved, how and when? Secondly, consider what specific attributes you bring to a managerial or professional role; how you relate to others, your interpersonal skills, your level of control, confidence, independence and zest for achievement. Then assess how far these identify you as a high performer, a moderate performer or a low performer. Do this by trying to measure various outcomes such as how far you meet or exceed targets, achieve team or corporate objectives, develop sound customer relationships, heighten your own reputation.

■ *Tip 2* – Develop your learning curve to its maximum efficiency. Treat learning as continuous and as a vital part of your market value and employability. Instead of repeating a set of limited experiences, broaden these so that you acquire new skills and knowledge. Learn from different sources such as customers, colleagues, conferences, databases, internet, intranets, bulletin boards, seminars and training courses; keep up to date with journals and professional literature.

- *Tip 3* — Build and manage your own intellectual capital. This consists of your specific skills and competencies, your experience, your ways of doing things. Not only do these add value to any role you undertake. By leveraging them you can produce benefits such as cost savings, speedier ways of working, increased productivity, improved problem solving. In particular, consider the value in a changing labour market of your transferable skills — how you plan, lead, listen, tackle problems, determine priorities, how you manage yourself, your time, your team. Establish a self-development plan to broaden and improve these as well as enhancing your numeracy and computing skills. Continually ask yourself, what does the market want and do I have plenty of it?
- *Tip 4* — Periodically review your career plan. If your career needs revitalising, see how far you can do this through job redesign, or through lateral transfers, or secondment to a customer, or even a short sabbatical in a university. Again, as long term security and stable employment declines, be aware of the need to face major career redirection more frequently. Consider the likely effect on your current or next role of such issues as changes in technology and structure, in reporting arrangements and senior managerial appointments, in fashion or markets, in legislation or a change of ownership. All these can seriously affect individual career aspirations. You should endeavour to have a contingency plan in place if you have to move on. Mobility, along with flexibility and adaptability to new environments will become one of the hallmarks of successful managers and professionals in the future.

WHAT'S HAPPENING TO ORGANISATIONS?

Over the last ten to fifteen years, the pace of change has virtually transformed the landscape of traditional organisations.

We have already seen that careers have been severely affected as a result of such drivers as downsizing, restructuring, technological developments, globalisation and intense competition. These same drivers are combining to bring about significant developments in organisations. It's not just traditional hierarchies being flattened. Many firms are now experimenting with quite radical designs. Matrix structures and loose networks replace slowly moving bureaucracies. These in turn create very different management processes, which emphasise the need for innovation, flexibility and continual adaptability. All these help them to meet the demands of turbulent and uncertain markets. There is far greater emphasis now on joint ventures, on the formation of strategic partnerships, on research consortia, outsourcing and decentralisation. Mergers, acquisitions, repositioning, divestments and buy-outs have become everyday currency. Employers rely far less on maintaining a large, permanent workforce. Extracting more productivity out of fewer people becomes the name of the game.

These trends not only affect the nature of the work we do. They also impact upon the kind of workforce needed and the nature of the workplace. Let us examine three particular issues surrounding organisational change which will continue to affect your job hunting activities both now and in the future.

Changes in management structures

Delayering, downsizing and the move towards fewer *core* and more *non-core* workers mean that decision making and the delegation of authority is driven downwards. Reporting hierarchies are streamlined and this transforms managerial ratios, with large numbers of middle managers being displaced. Managers who remain after restructuring tend to find their competencies coming under greater scrutiny as the organisation seeks greater profitability. Their individual workloads and personal responsibilities also increase as tiers are removed and command and controls systems are de-emphasised. In some cases this can bring personal benefits because their range of skills broadens, thus making them more marketable. The critical feature of restructuring is that it alters the internal labour market, affecting jobs and promotion opportunities. At the same time it changes the demand for certain skills and experience. Such things as titles and tasks, divisions and departments, become reshaped and redesigned. The operating environment is also altered while personal relationships readjust to the new reality. By their very nature these issues affect the morale, motivation and the long term commitment of those who survive after such drastic developments. A delicate balance begins to emerge between your own individual security and the need for the firm to remain flexible.

You will need to assess how far these changes in management structures will affect your opportunities for promotion and individual development. If you are targeting a recently restructured organisation, consider the ways in which the new arrangements will alter the balance of power and control. Think also about possible changes in reporting procedures, and if resources are in place to enable you to grow and increase your autonomy and overall prospects. You may also bear in mind how the changes affect recruitment and selection (for example, delegated to line managers rather than personnel): how they impact on communication, on team development as well as the overall corporate culture.

Changes in new technology

Technological development is frequently referred to as the driving force of most organisational change. It particularly affects the design of operations; for example, local area networks are critical in supporting decentralisation. IT developments can clearly alter the ways in which you are likely to be recruited and selected. Consider, for example, the growth of scannable CVs, cyberspace recruitment on the Internet, and the use of specialised databases by headhunters. At the same time, IT developments have brought about the rise of teleworkers, with far fewer managers and professionals working on a standard 9 to 5 basis. The merging of computers and telephones, the growth of networking and digital systems, and the increasing influence of multi-media will all combine to dramatically alter the context of the workplace for many managers and professionals. You will no longer be bound to work in a specified place at a specified time. Instead your work will be less defined by location and more by your connectivity to information technology. This will involve you not only being fully conversant and at ease with the technology, but also being aware of its impact on your own skills and productivity. Take a little time to assess the likely effect on jobs and the workplace over the next decade of robotics, artificial intelligence, expert systems and object oriented databases, to name but a few! You may have your own 'pet list' to consider.

What is important, in terms of your own job hunting and career prospects, is to analyse how technology may affect the *nature of the work you do*, both now and in the future; for example

- it can have a dramatic effect on the specific tasks or jobs you perform (making them easier, performed faster and better, even eliminated);
- it can alter how your job is configured and how you interact and relate to other colleagues;
- it can alter the context and organisation of your work (location, reporting and control systems).

An important part of the debate about technology is the extent to which it creates or destroys jobs. Certainly those industries which are related to IT are among the fastest growing in global terms and are the source of a vast number of new jobs. Indeed, the development of IT is a crucial part of the movement towards the *knowledge-based economy*. Although we see in this economy an increase in the demand for highly skilled people, at the same time many skills could become obsolete very quickly. IT clearly has the potential to destroy work opportunities as innovation in production reduces the demand for labour per unit of output. Whatever your role, you should continually assess the impact of new technology on the way it affects the nature and organisation of the work you do as well as the skill requirements of your particular job and profession. You have only to look at the current emphasis on teamwork, network-building, and continuous learning to realise these are in response to pressures to become leaner in production, to improve quality and customer care, and to develop new forms of organisation.

The rise of the learning organisation

This brief section on the learning organisation has been specifically included because the concept is now regarded in the late 1990s as one of the hot areas of management education. Much has been written about the need for organisations to respond quickly and positively so that they can survive as well as prosper in an unpredictable and often hostile business world. You may already be highly aware of, and experienced in, such initiatives as TQM, Business Process Re-engineering, Benchmarking or JIT. All these have been tried so that organisations can deliver continuous improvement, or gain competitive advantage or meet and exceed customer needs. The idea of the learning organisation is that these initiatives in themselves are not enough to bring about the transformation of firms so that they can readily adapt to rapid and unexpected change. In reply to the question 'why develop a learning organisation'?, Mabey and Iles in *Managing Learning*, put it very succinctly. 'It is not that "learning" has been without its advocates, rather that the message seems finally to have got through that it is an essential strand of commercial flexibility, employee empowerment and personal fulfilment in the work setting.' Supporters of the learning organisation take the view that if businesses want to be successful in responding to uncertainty, then a very different, almost holistic approach is needed.

Out goes the idea that you can cope and adapt merely by

cutting costs, exerting rigid controls and installing top-down management preoccupied with systems and processes. In comes a heightened emphasis on generating ideas, on innovation and creativity, on building a culture in which individuals, teams and the whole organisation continually interact and learn together. Underpinning this approach (which is not without its critics) is the development of much higher levels of knowledge and skills within the workforce. This is because the management processes within the learning organisation demand considerable expertise in such areas as strategic planning, competitor analysis, information resource management, groupware processes, organisation development and performance measurement. All this requires considerable effort on the part of managers and professionals in learning new skills and in taking an active part in developing their own capabilities as well as their team colleagues. The old division between employers and workers is replaced by managers and knowledge workers whose joint goal is to collaborate to create what has been termed *the knowledge-creating company*.

Clearly from this brief overview you will appreciate that the learning organisation offers a very different environment and set of challenges from traditional mechanistic and bureaucratic firms. It is one which does not accept command and control, nor does it assume that past success will deliver future prosperity. Instead, because decisions are based on expertise rather than status and power, they can be invigorating and exciting places in which to work. Indeed, there is clear evidence that this will be the preferred route for many growth-oriented organisations to follow in the next decade or more. Put simply, learning is no longer seen as a choice but as a necessity. You strive to learn faster, smarter and better or you are out of business.

If your job hunting is directed towards securing a position in a learning organisation, then you will need to ask yourself three important questions.

1. Are your current skills and credentials sufficiently up-to-date and relevant to enable you to make a significant contribution to the knowledge base of the organisation?

2. Do you have a strong commitment to continuous learning, problem solving, mentoring and coaching, exchanging information and ideas, backed by tangible evidence of your creativity and innovation in your previous work?
3. Is your personality such that you will relish experimentation, thrive on ambiguity and uncertainty, be capable of learning from failure, and take responsibility for your own self-development?

If your response to all three questions is a resounding *yes*, then the learning organisation may well be the place where you are likely to find your *best fit*.

WHAT'S HAPPENING TO WORK AND JOBS?

As a manager or professional, you may occasionally ask yourself why you work. Over a period of time you are likely to come up with several different reasons. You have a need for income and security; you feel work can give you personal recognition as well as a sense of social identity (you are what you do or where you work). Work may also give you some self-satisfaction and enable you to be recognised by others. It may provide challenge and interest and give you a feeling you are doing something valuable and constructive with your life.

Many of these feelings and attitudes stem from our experience in the traditional workplace. Here job responsibilities are well defined, while rules and procedures are clearly set out. The job itself is the building block of the organisation and the main vehicle for accomplishing work. At the same time we are expected to work. We are socialised to look for work and to keep our jobs. Anything which threatens our ego or security at work becomes highly important to us.

However, significant changes are now affecting the workplace. Already we have discussed some of the implications of changes in structure and technology. These are part of the reason why many of our earlier expectations and assumptions about the workplace are rapidly being replaced. Charles Handy put this in a nutshell when asked who would remain in the executive goldfish bowl after these changes had worked their way through. 'We will have half the number of managers, paid twice as much, and expected to be three times more productive.'

To give you a clearer idea of how the workplace is altering, let us examine three more distinct issues widely seen as 'drivers of change'. These are set out below.

Examples of drivers of change within the workplace

- *Patterns of Work* – Increased emphasis on core and non-core workers; movement towards fixed term contracts/job sharing; rise in number of self-employed, especially among women; by 2000 over 50 per cent of the UK workforce will be women. Greater use of temporary executives; sharp increase in working from home/telecottages; only 30 per cent work Monday to Friday on a 9–5 basis; about 10 per cent of jobs in the E.C. 'die' each year.
- *Attitudes to Work* – Corporate loyalty affected by fears of job security; belief in the job for life rapidly disappearing. Increased mobility of knowledge workers especially in IT. Less dependency on, and trust in, a single employer.
- *Psychological Contract* – More emphasis on becoming employable, not employed; careers becoming boundary-less, with periodic reskilling. Managers changing jobs, companies and careers more often. Increased use of interim managers – outsourcing of skills.

Before moving on to assess how far these changes affect jobs, why not pose an interesting question? As a manager or professional, do you really need an office, with all its attendant costs? With a mobile phone (digital, of course), a high entry level laptop with supporting software and e-mail, a fax, pager, scanner and answerphone, you could argue that the office as we know it becomes far less significant. You will certainly find that such developments will leave you more flexible; with less interruptions you could be more productive. But do travel savings and reduced stress levels necessarily bring greater benefits when you are cut off from office gossip and politics?

We have looked at some of the changes affecting the workplace. Let us now briefly consider what is also happening to jobs. Already there is strong evidence that it is small to medium sized firms which add to the pool of jobs, while large ones tend to take away or at best add very little. Where jobs will come from in the future is always an interesting question, and is influenced by three main factors.

1. First, there are changes in the composition and movement of the population (increased proportion of elderly people, variations in birth rates in different areas, geographical shifts with urban decline and rural growth). These will clearly affect the demand for goods and services. We are highly likely to want more housing, more education, more health provision, more care and support services. At the same time jobs in hotel and catering, in business and personal services, and telecommunications are set to rise.

2. Secondly, there are changes in the size and age distribution of the labour force (more people retiring earlier, more diversity in the workplace, more women and graduates entering the labour market and more people endeavouring to improve their credentials and skill levels). While the UK labour force is estimated to grow to almost 30 million by 2006, most of this growth will come from women in part-time jobs in small firms with fewer than 100 employees.

3. Thirdly, there are changes in occupational structure. Less skilled jobs will continue to disappear. New jobs will be created in skills-intensive and knowledge-based occupations, predominantly in services and manufacturing. To give you an idea of the extent of change in occupations, the 1940 edition of *The Dictionary of Occupational Titles* listed over 30,000 jobs, most of which had disappeared by 1997. The *London Post Office Directory* of 1900 listed blood dryers, lamplighters and soot merchants. These are a far

cry from new jobs such as ATM technicians, silicon chip inspectors and database developers.

Where new jobs will come from, what they will demand in terms of skills and experience, and what they will offer in career and personal prospects will be an important issue for managers and professionals. It will be especially significant if you need to change careers as a result of redundancy or because you see your current prospects either distinctly limited or positively declining. As the skills content of many managerial and professional roles change, the boundaries between occupations and the qualifications which set them apart will become much less clear. What is now rapidly emerging is a class or group commonly referred to as *knowledge workers*. Their development and continued employability will be conditional on continuous learning and keeping up to date with job and work related skills.

In the same ways in which the workplace is transforming, so is our notion of the traditional stable job. The various changes we have already discussed are rapidly altering our assumptions of what actually constitutes a job (such as its tasks and activities, or the behaviour and skills needed to perform it effectively). As old jobs disappear and new ones emerge (eg web page designers), the very stability of jobs is being seriously challenged. In the past, the job was regarded as the stable building block of the organisation. It was defined and described. It was given a title, it had duties, responsibilities and purpose and it was measured and rewarded. Around the job the organisation managed its activities and designed its structure. This is no longer so. Pressures to downsize and restructure, to decentralise and become leaner and flatter, have in turn led firms to put greater emphasis on multi-skilling, on self-directed teams, on flexibility and adaptability. It has been calculated by Charles Handy that a job which lasted 100,000 hours a generation ago could now be achieved in about 10,000 hours. In less than a decade this could fall to 1000 hours as technology alters the speed of work.

The combined effect of these developments is that you are less likely to be selected to undertake a specific job. Instead you will be seen and valued as a knowledge worker with a set of skills and behaviours designed to accomplish tasks and assignments within teams and on a project basis. Just as the project changes over time, so will your responsibilities and the tasks you undertake. Your aim will be to do the work which needs to be done, not to perform in a job with defined boundaries and responsibilities. At the same time, be aware that many of the skills you exercise at work will have a distinct 'shelf-life'. They will need constant evaluation as the organisation you work for confronts changing situations and environments. Even your 'core skills', like creativity and imagination, problem solving and decision-making, planning and communicating, will all require periodic reassessment if you are to be seen as a successful performer, especially within a learning organisation. Your aim will be to respond to the realities of the labour market. You will find yourself changing functions, responsibilities and employers as your career is devoted far less to a single occupation.

Here are two suggestions which are designed to help you to adjust to this 'new reality'.

1. Think about how you can *benchmark* your skills against your competitors. What do you need to do to continually make yourself attractive to employers? What can you bring to market which others can't do yet? What performance standards should you set yourself to keep ahead of the opposition?

2. Look at how you can *reinvent or renew yourself* (rather like the way learning organisations cope with discontinuous change). What will it take to revitalise the way you do things: how will this affect your performance? From what will you derive your authority in the future – is it your position, or your leadership, or your team building and motivating skills, or your interpersonal competencies? How will you anticipate future trends in your business; can you handle crisis, rumours, sudden departures, media attention, hostile bids or unexpected profits warnings?

WHAT'S HAPPENING TO MODERN JOB HUNTING STRATEGIES?

It is when you come to designing and implementing your job hunting strategy that you begin to see the importance of the *symbiotic relationship* between the *content* and the *context* of your job search. Much of the advice on the *content* of systematic job search follows fairly traditional lines. In other words, it describes the various steps you should go through.

■ Read several books or articles concerned with the 'how to' of job search.
■ Develop your CV and covering letters.
■ Scan papers and journals for likely advertised vacancies; despatch CVs and letters.
■ Compile list of potential employers and send out a batch of unsolicited letters and CVs.
■ Develop contacts with agencies and recruiters; activate your network and signal your availability.
■ Attend interviews; if offered a position, evaluate the offer, discuss terms and starting date.

This basic outline seems logical and straightforward, but it is too simplistic and mechanical. Essentially, it ignores the other half of the equation, namely the changing *context* of modern job hunting. In other words, your own personal success will greatly depend on what's happening within the environment in which jobs, work and careers are set and developed.

Here are three suggestions to help you design your job hunting so that it is far more in tune with these rapidly changing environments which we have already discussed.

1. Analyse what changes in the structure and design of organisations are likely to mean to you. Their populations or demography will continue to ebb and flow. Resignations, retirements, redundancies, promotions, departures and deaths will affect not only the occupational profile but also the internal labour market. In the same way, organic growth, the winning of sizeable contracts, breakthroughs

in new technology are all positive signs which should be noted for future reference. As new jobs are created and old ones removed, the shape of the organisation changes (it may move from pyramidal to onion shaped). A window of opportunity may quickly appear and just as quickly be filled by someone who is in the right place at the right time. Whatever you may think of a company as a potential target or useful prospect, it will be your task to find out as much as possible about these issues. This means keeping up to date with trends, developments, market movements, analysts reports, statements and results. Journals, newspapers and the trade press are all useful sources. Senior appointments or departures can herald opportunities if they lead to changes in teams and goals. Find out about selection procedures and how far an organisation 'grows its own' or imports from the market when needed. Knowing how long people at your level stay, and why they leave is all valuable information in assessing your prospects. Also look for danger signs when organisations may be heading for trouble; passing a dividend, profit warnings, diving share price, abrupt departures, loss of major contracts and customers, lack of investment and late creditor payments are all tell-tale signs of declining performance. If your expertise is in turnarounds and rejuvenation, these will be of real interest.

2. Determine what you want out of the job or the work you will be doing. Pose some searching questions. How far is job satisfaction, tenure, security and autonomy important to you? How important is the job within the structure and will you have the chance to grow and develop it? Are the rewards and remuneration sufficiently attractive and an accurate guide to your worth? Are there hidden stresses in the job and can you handle these? Does the job match your skills, personal preferences and fit in with your personal or family circumstances? Will you need to make a speedy transition into the new role; are you clear about how you will be rated and what your reporting arrangements will involve. In particular, find out what attracts you to a

particular job or organisation. Is it to do with culture, reputation, prestige or values as you see them? Do you have enough information on these to make a sound decision?

3.   Consider the ways in which you can fit into an organisation. You will need to find out about what the organisation is actually like, its personality and prevailing work climate and if it is in the process of transformation. You may be keen to get on board a hard driving, rigorous and results-oriented firm, or one which has a high growth potential and ambitious future plans. Then you should discover what is going on in the team(s) you are likely to join. As work teams increase in use and importance, especially in flatter organisations, this will be an important issue for you. Factors such as the teams' goals, record, leadership, relationships, attitudes, composition and skills mix, need to be weighed up. Finally, you should look at the tasks you are expected to accomplish. Will these stretch and invigorate or leave you stressed and debilitated? For many successful candidates entering a new organisation, there is often a mismatch between how they perceive fitting in and how they actually fit in. In some cases this can lead to an early departure, especially if you misjudge the prevailing climate or your skills are very 'firm specific' and not easily transferable. It is therefore vital that you examine the basis of your decision to join a particular firm. Do not simply rely on its reputation or its status and rewards package. Instead, carefully dig behind the image of the organisation to find out how far it matches your own personality. In some cases you may prefer ambitious, rigorous and tough workplaces which fit in with your own competitiveness and need for achievement. Others may opt for something more serene and tranquil, more secure and less commercial. Whatever your preferences, assessing how you will fit in is a most important aspect of your job hunting. Hitting the right balance will give you a far better opportunity to achieve higher levels of job satisfaction, improve your performance and heighten your commitment.

These examples (and there are more to follow in later chapters) demonstrate why you need to integrate both the content and context of job hunting to improve your overall effectiveness. Far better to adopt a broader and more considered perspective than to take a job which in the event turns out to be a 'career limiting move'.

2

Becoming a Successful Job Hunter: Your Smart Guide to Planning, Marketing and Research

INTRODUCTION

In Chapter One, we built a basic picture of the successful organisation of the future. It is sensitive to, and learns from, changes in its environment. It seizes new opportunities by keeping adaptable and flexible. It is not afraid to reinvent itself. If you then ask yourself what this is likely to mean for your own job and career, then the analogy is quite clear. You will need to react in a very similar fashion. Your own flexibility and mobility will be translated into an increasing number of job changes and the prospect of two or more career changes over your working lifetime.

By the start of the next century, job changing will become an even more important part of corporate life. In the same context, job mobility is set to assume greater significance in the working lives of managers and professionals. In some cases, you may be in a position to plan your next job change and your move will be voluntary and clearly thought out. You move because you want extra responsibility, or to widen your experience, or you're keen to find a more supportive and innovative culture. However, many job and career changes are not like that. They arrive suddenly and often without warning. These are the involuntary changes which arise from company failure or also from redundancy, often the result of mergers, downsizing or even the arrival of a new boss. When this happens and you are unprepared, panic may set in and you become confused and unclear what to do next.

This is where this book is designed to help. For much of the background to it arises from a range of concerns expressed by experienced search and selection consultants, outplacement specialists, career counsellors, selectors and writers on job search. Put simply, they confirm that to remain employable in the future, managers and professionals will need to improve considerably their job hunting skills and strategies. These concerns are illustrated as follows:

- 'nine out of ten candidates failed to appreciate the value of impression management at the interview and then compounded this by performing miserably when making their presentations'
- 'when asked if they had a defined marketing plan and a clear grasp of how to research companies, markets and products through databases and the Internet, less than 10 per cent knew what we were on about'
- 'most of the people were plain rusty – poorly prepared for the rigours of the initial panel interview, and the searching one-to-one with the Chairman left them all gasping'
- 'so many of the middle managers who come through my door are over reliant on their previous organisation as a safe haven; if they do have transferable skills, they certainly can't sell them'
- 'there is no excuse now for professionals to be unaware of the rapid changes affecting the labour market or to say their kind of skills will always be wanted, because they won't'
- 'when I asked the people on the short list what they had done for their own self-development over the last twelve months, all said they had been to a one-day conference in Harrogate'

Even from this small sample, it does appear that more has to be achieved in terms of job hunting skills by those managers and professionals who may be faced with redundancy and career change. It is equally significant for high achievers or those who may be returning to the labour market after a layoff, or after retraining, or through family considerations.

Please do not regard job hunting in today's competitive climate as an ordeal or an insuperable hurdle, because it clearly is not. Already, there is a wide range of support and advice available to you. Job clubs, career advisors, recruitment agencies, outplacement consultants, government schemes and chartered psychologists all vie with each other to help you in different ways and with varying results. For your part, it does mean considerable effort, coupled with a high degree of energy and tenacity. Indeed, there is much hard evidence to support the view that those who work harder and expend greater effort, perform far better in their job hunting. Much of this is linked to how conscientious you are; in other words, ask yourself if you have the will to achieve as well as the discipline and organisational skills to sustain yourself during job hunting. At the same time weigh up if you are dependable, organised, thorough and careful in your approach.

What we are emphasising is that there are several tried and trusted ways to improve your preparedness so that you become more confident and self-assured. As we stressed in Chapter One, much of your activity will focus on your self-marketing, your networking and your impression management, all critical issues which are fully developed throughout this book. Becoming innovative and creative can also reap rich dividends. Let us give two examples. Recently a displaced senior executive did something different to overcome what he felt was a problem with his age (he was 52). He distributed over 1000 copies of his one-page CV on the windscreens of expensive cars in a large city centre car park. He managed to secure three good offers within one month and accepted one which really fitted his skills and aspirations. Again, a woman marketing manager produced, via the Internet, a very well designed web page of her recent successes and was overwhelmed with the response. She took up a directorship of a small but fast growing software house soon afterwards.

EXAMINING WHAT LIES BEHIND YOUR JOB HUNTING

Several motives may lie behind your job hunting. For example, you may start searching because:

- You are currently dissatisfied and feel uncomfortable, undervalued, stressed and somewhat insecure. Promotion seems unlikely and there is a danger you will find yourself plateaued or passed over
- You are using it to build up your existing network of influential contacts, letting them know of your future availability and testing reactions to your enquiries.
- You are signalling to your present organisation that it may lose you unless it improves your current conditions or rewards.
- You are scanning opportunities not only to test your market value, but also to explore possible openings into new roles in case of a sudden departure (often a reaction to rumours of change).
- You have been declared redundant and need to find another position as soon as possible.

Your motives will certainly exert an important influence on your job hunting. Alongside these you will also need to determine what are your career values since these affect what you are aiming for. This will be especially useful during your networking or in discussions with search and selection consultants. For example, you may aspire in your career to reach top management, or you may seek independence, thus freeing yourself from the control and supervision of others. Again, you may be looking for a position which can offer security rather than risk, or one which enables you to be creative, original and innovative.

BECOMING A SUCCESSFUL JOB HUNTER

Underpinning your job hunting, and as a basis for your future success, you will need to address five basic questions.

1. *What is your overall strategy?* You will need to determine if this is to be random, and very broad. By looking at the big picture you begin to identify where the jobs are now and where they are set to grow. This helps you identify as many opportunities as you can. Or it could be highly focused and very restricted, where you have narrowed the field to a specific industry and location. In addition you will need to decide what you are looking for and how feasible this is in the current labour market.

2. *How do you intend to search?* Here you will have to decide which methods are best suited to your needs, what kind of approaches bring good results, and how comfortable you are with your chosen method (eg networking, or contacting agencies and selection consultants, or direct targeting of selected employers, or answering adverts).

3. *Why are you adopting a particular approach?* This involves you taking a critical look at your search methods and determining the background to your choice. It may depend on your existing knowledge and awareness of job search, or because traditionally you have always approached the problem in a certain way. For example, you could find networking difficult and you may prefer to deal at arm's length through advertisements or agencies. However, what worked well last time may not necessarily be appropriate the next time round. Online search may be the way forward next time.

4. *When do you intend to search?* You will need to assess not only the time you have available, but whether your search is immediate or could be conducted later on. If your search is spasmodic and intermittent, then you should establish reasons for your timing and market yourself accordingly.

5. *Where do you intend to search?* You will be faced with a choice of sector or industry, geographic location, home or

abroad, as well as discipline or profession. This is likely to involve substantial research in well stocked libraries, and online, over a longer period of time.

Other choices include how much effort you intend to give to your search, and over how long a period. You may need to decide how many offers to gather before making a final decision. That too will need to be based on some predetermined standard to minimise the risk of making a poor choice.

Another innovative way of tackling your job hunting is to ask yourself a basic but vital question: *'what do I do to become a successful candidate now and for the rest of my working life?'*

If you turn to specialists in the field, you will usually receive some fairly standard replies, eg *If you want to make a success of changing your job or career, you need to be highly organised, good at research and have a self-marketing plan which works.*

You will only get where you want if you show staying power, commitment and confidence, and can handle rejection and discrimination on the way.

Before you start, analyse your career goals, set yourself clear objectives, develop a winning attitude, and above all take the initiative.

It all depends on your network contacts, on how you develop your image and impress others.

While all these seem sound advice, you may have reservations about your enthusiasm or skill to make 'things happen', You may regard yourself as 'rusty' and out of practice. Put simply, these are negative feelings which will hinder your progress. For all of us have something to offer which can be valuable, creative and influential. Therefore, start with the very positive notion that you have within yourself the capabilities and potential to make a rewarding job move or career change. If your human capital is better and more relevant than other candidates, then you are more attractive to employers. This increases your chances of landing the job you want.

DEVELOPING YOUR MARKETING PLAN

Much of your job hunting will centre around three main activities:

■ *collecting and exchanging information* – in the form of CVs and letters, telemarketing, going for interviews, data analysis and communicating your knowledge and experience;
■ *selling your services* – as a specialist knowledge worker offering your skills and experience as solutions to customers' problems;
■ *establishing contacts* – through networking, information interviews, library research, the Internet.

These activities, which are covered in detail in subsequent chapters, form an important part of your overall marketing strategy. But before you can effectively put them into operation, you will need to establish a basic but well-thought-out marketing plan, which you can then review and develop as you progress. You can visualise this in the following format:

Establishing Your Objectives: *Your Statement of Purpose*	*Developing Your Tools and Techniques:* *Your Means of Achieving Your Purpose*
Determining your career goals	Undertaking research and market intelligence
Deciding how and what to develop	Selling, promoting and advertising yourself
Examining the opportunities available	Enhancing your presentation and publicity
Creating a demand for your services	Negotiating your rewards and remuneration
Adding value through ideas, energy, time	Establishing your reputation and expertise
Satisfying customers by solving problems	Engaging in professional self-development

Within your marketing plan, you will need to establish a clear relationship between the objectives you are setting yourself and the tools and techniques you use to achieve them. For example, your career goals are likely to change as you get older and you could move from full-time to self-employment. Again you may decide to go into sub-contracting, or become an interim-executive, or develop your own business or consultancy. Different career goals demand different techniques. Often the higher you progress the greater the importance of your interpersonal and behavioural skills as opposed to your professional or technical expertise.

You will also need to decide whether you change industry or sector, what is transferable about your skills, how far you will relocate if needed, how you intend to target prospects and what particular environment will best suit your personality. Doubtless you will construct a much larger list of key issues. In your marketing plan you will also need to take account of the nature of the job market and adopt your tools and techniques accordingly. Essentially, you can divide the job market (a place where buyers and sellers come together and where you go to discover jobs) into four main segments.

1. Jobs which arise out of advertised vacancies published in a wide variety of newspapers, journals and the trade press, plus the Internet – these are in 'the public domain' and open for all to see.
2. Jobs which are available through search and selection consultants, as well as agencies and interim-manager specialists – these are far less open and form part of the 'hidden job market'.
3. Jobs which are not advertised and not on 'public show', but which you can find or even create through networking and developing personal contacts – again, these are part of the 'hidden job market'.
4. Jobs which you find through speculative approaches to targeted organisations, often resulting from your research and market intelligence activities – these are clearly 'hidden' from public view.

Look upon each segment as a different part of the overall job market, demanding different marketing skills and methods and at the same time, producing quite different results. Your aim will be to focus on each segment and to determine which approach is likely to produce the most profitable return.

CREATING YOUR PERSONAL DOSSIER

Creating a personal dossier is especially useful when you start job hunting. Develop your dossier both as evidence and as a permanent record of such things as your range and type of experience; what you have learned and need to learn in the future; what you have done to develop yourself; how well you perform in different roles; what you are aiming for and what contacts you have made to help you on the way. The following suggestions are designed to stimulate your interest and help you design your own dossier in the way which suits you best.

1. *What have you accomplished and achieved?* Give examples of projects, assignments, courses, credentials, awards, recommendations, updating of skills and competencies, training outcomes.
2. *What is your range and type of experience?* Show its nature and extent, what you have learned, how well was it learned, and how this has helped you to add value and perform better.
3. *What have you done for your professional development?* Indicate courses, credentials, research, special ventures, and any performance reviews or psychometric reports you have received.
4. *What is your marketing literature?* Prepare two or three differently designed CVs, which you update regularly and which accurately reflect your responsibilities and performance outcomes. Also include a set of covering letters, which you can use to respond to advertisements, for

networking, or to send to agencies and selection consultants.

5. *What is your personal network? Who are your contacts?* Compile a list of names, positions, clubs, associations, business cards etc. The chapter on networking will give you more ideas.

6. *Which specialist search and selection consultants, agencies, headhunters may be of help to you?*

7. Have you set up details of specialist services such as employment lawyers (in case of redundancy or dismissal), outplacement consultants (in case of termination when career counselling may be offered)?

8. Are you collecting clippings of interesting job adverts where you are likely to match the specification, or articles which give ideas and information relating to the role/organisation/sector you are seeking?

JOB CHANGE OR CAREER CHANGE?

We have already discussed the need for managers and professionals to adapt their jobs and careers to rapid and discontinuous change. Continually appraising your progress, updating your self development, while putting in place a contingency plan if things go wrong, will be important issues for you to consider. Compared with twenty five years ago, managerial mobility is much greater now as the pattern of employment and the structure of the labour market alters. Recent predictions suggest that by the beginning of the next century, many managers will be looking to work for at least ten employers over their working lifetime. This will certainly put your job hunting skills to the test!

You can visualise your own job mobility in different ways, eg you can change your present employer or your current job; you may find you have to move location, or assume different responsibilities. Again, you may move to a different type of industry and in the process you may find your status or position also changes. When it comes to career change, much of the movement is towards self-employment, especially for those in the 35–50 age group. You may look upon self-employment as an opportunity to do something you always longed to do, with greater personal freedom and satisfaction.

Whether you are considering changing your job, or going a step further and changing your career, you will have to face some important issues. *Job change* often requires you to use similar skills, knowledge and range of contacts you have built up in your previous job. While your transition into the new role may not be dramatic, you will still need to undertake a critical assessment of yourself and your abilities, eg:

- How do you propose to fit into the new work culture and be accepted into the new workplace?
- What changes will you need to make to ensure you hit it off with your new boss?
- How will you adapt to a new work team, new procedures and invariably new management styles?
- Are you clear about the new targets to be met and the expectations people have of you?
- Will your current skill levels need updating or revitalising to ensure you remain employable?
- What is the likely impact on domestic arrangements or family routines, or your social network?

When it comes to *career change*, you are invariably entering a different world. Not only will you have to give it very careful thought; it will also involve a rigorous appraisal of the risks and opportunities involved. Because the transition is that much greater, here are some key factors for you to put into your plan.

- What reasons lie behind your proposed career change; are they driven by fear of redundancy or need for greater security, or are you looking to run your own show on your own terms?
- Will a career change enable you to reach your full potential and achieve higher rewards?

- Have you analysed the financial risks and long-term implications for your future and your dependants?
- What special new skills will you need to acquire and will you be able to cope with the workload?
- Are you able to make the financial adjustment to your living standards if you need to retrain?
- Will there be openings for you once you have completed your training?
- Are you psychologically prepared to adjust to a new work ethic and new work environment?
- Do you have the necessary support, understanding and co-operation from others to make it a success?
- Have you the personality factors, such as drive, motivation and commitment, to adjust to a new career?
- Do you have the ability and influence to build new networks in order to establish your reputation?
- Given your track record, are you confident you can manage new forms of stress which may arise?
- Have you separated your desire for change from the opportunities which are actually available?

Career change, as you will appreciate from these rather searching questions, is much more dramatic and has far-reaching consequences. It can bring you excitement and exhilaration. Or it may produce fear and possible failure. You will not be alone in giving it serious thought. Many managers and professionals make the successful transition. Much will depend on your ability to manage the risks (financial and psychological) and to ensure that whatever new career path you choose is in line with your needs, values, skills and abilities.

THE IMPORTANCE OF LIBRARY RESEARCH

If your job hunting is to be successful, then much will hinge on your research abilities and the quality of background information you can obtain. Larger public libraries, especially in large cities or county headquarters, along with university, business school and even government department libraries, are rich and interesting sources of information. In your work plan, find out your nearest good libraries and check on membership details, especially for university libraries. Then set out to learn their layout and indexing, the extent of their source material, their special collections or expertise, their opening hours and any technical or online facilities they can provide.

To increase your credibility and to enhance your prospects you cannot rely simply on your experience. If you are to impress, whether networking, making presentations, sending speculative letters or being interviewed, you need to do your homework. If, like many managers and professionals, you are looking ahead to a job change in the next two years or so, that means keeping in touch with what is happening in organisations, and in particular sectors. It also implies you should be keenly aware of issues affecting the surrounding business and professional environment. To do this effectively, you will need to develop a curious and enquiring attitude, as well as becoming highly organised and efficient in using library resources and Internet facilities.

Let us look at three levels of job hunting activity where your research skills are especially important.

■ First, researching a particular sector or type of industry; this could be in distribution, retailing, professional services, health, education, food, computing. You may need to find out about economic developments, growth prospects, emerging trends, competitive pressures, technological influences, mergers and acquisitions, legislative changes, skills and labour requirements, etc. Research here will give you a feel for likely openings; who are the key players, who is on the move, what skills and experiences are in demand.

■ Secondly, researching a particular organisation; this could involve finding out about products or services, current and past financial performance, annual reports, market share, current marketing and advertising, managerial changes, contracts awarded, analysts' views, research and development plans, number of employees, location of operations, board members, contact names, addresses and telephone numbers.

■ Thirdly, researching particular jobs, occupations or careers, depending on your future plans. This may involve you finding out about new jobs that are emerging, entry requirements for professions, training facilities for self-development, advanced courses in universities, as well as skill needs and career prospects in the future.

Whether you are responding to an advertisement which gives the organisation's name, or alternatively sending a speculative or networking letter, sound research doesn't just indicate your interest. It also gives clues to your level of preparedness and your commitment to work in a particular sector or company. Research also becomes even more significant when you are asked to make a presentation, or to attend an interview.

Since large libraries contain a vast amount of information, you may be forgiven if you find there is so much that you don't know where to start. Much depends on your research skills and how motivated you are to spend time finding journals, searching indexes, scouring databases, reading and photocopying. Here are four ideas to help you make sense of your research.

1. Visit two or three libraries to assess how far they will be able to help you. Obtain as much information as possible on their services. Spend time browsing and make a note of any special sources you find valuable. If they have a special commercial section, this will be particularly useful. Check on their holdings of journals, company reports, quality newspapers, Extel and McCarthy cards, overseas information, online facilities. Explain the purpose of your visit to qualified staff in Information Sciences, who can be a valuable source of advice.

2. Whenever you visit, have a defined purpose in mind. Focus on what you want to find out by preparing a list of questions you want answering. Then set out what kind of

information you need (should it be old or new data, practical or theoretical, primary or secondary, highly technical or just general). Then establish the best source of information, and order it from inter-library loan if not immediately to hand.

3. Make sure your research is well organised. Set up a special research folder, with an index of the material you collect. Develop an ongoing bibliography of books, reference sources, journals, databases and anything which identifies where to find relevant material. Keep cuttings, photocopies, statistics, quotations, file cards, interview notes, presentation ideas, ideas for networking discussions, brochures, marketing literature. Go through journals in your specialist area and scan them for articles, job adverts, seminar and conference reports, commercial promotions, product news, latest appointments.

4. Learn to use computer databases, which are a fast and efficient way of locating information. They are less tedious than undertaking a manual search. If you are paying for access, they are more expensive. Select those databases which will give you the most appropriate data; enter key words and print out sources and summaries of what you need. Useful ones include *OCLC, BIDS-UNCOVER, DIALOG, Comtex, Keynote, Duns Marketing Online, Management and Marketing Abstracts, TDS Business File*. Specialist librarians trained in database information retrieval will be able to guide you through the maze.

To give you a flavour of what is available, here is a brief selection of reference works which are especially useful for job hunters:

Key British Enterprises
The Times 1000 Leading
  Companies
Kompass UK
The Research Index
Kelly's Business and Regional
  Directories

Stock Exchange Official Yearbook
Who Owns Whom
FAME – a database of company
  information
Directory of British Associations
Hambro Company Guide
Mintel

British Companies Index
Current British Directories
The Personnel Manager's
   Yearbook
The Source Book

The Executive Grapevine
Sources of European Economic
   Information
Extel Financial Analyst Services

TELEMARKETING YOURSELF

Using the telephone is a vital part of your overall marketing strategy. Not only is the telephone important in your market research; it is an essential tool in optimising your business and networking contacts because you use it to generate leads and make interesting appointments. Along with your marketing literature, it is the means by which you signal your interest and enhance awareness of yourself. Whatever your feelings and reservations, telemarketing is one of the main means by which you can effectively promote yourself as a valuable asset to a potential employer.

You will find the telephone invaluable in helping you to respond quickly and cost effectively to a job opportunity. It offers you a high degree of personal flexibility and enables you to target a prospect in a very precise way. It can be especially good in opening doors and establishing personal contact. In this sense, it shows that you are not afraid to take the initiative or to be proactive rather than reactive in your job search. You are portrayed as someone who seizes opportunities rather than waits for them to happen. By means of your voice, your verbal fluency and the ways in which you describe your achievements or expertise (often to a complete stranger) you can project your image at an early stage in your job search.

For many selectors like to hear what you say and the way you say it before they agree to see you. Letters cannot do this in the same way. It is through telemarketing that you can gain and impart crucial information, while at the same time showing your persuasiveness and persistence. It is an integral part of your overall impression management.

Having said that, there is plenty of evidence to suggest that many managers and professionals often fail to explore the real potential of telemarketing. On a personal level, you may feel uncomfortable in establishing instant rapport with a stranger. You would prefer to start with a targeted letter and then open up in a face to face discussion. You may consider it is not really a professional way to conduct your job search because it smacks of cold canvassing and opportunism. You may fear rejection from an assertive and overprotective personal assistant or you are fobbed off with someone who is not interested and can't make hiring decisions. Even when you reach your 'target', you may 'blow it' because you do not have the special communication skills to put your message across quickly, succinctly and persuasively. Overall, it may seem far too speculative and chancy to be important; far better to send your CV and covering letter and then wait to see what happens.

You are not alone in raising these quite valid objections. What has to be stressed is that, like many who have gone before you, you can overcome them by careful planning and preparation. Here are five ways which can help to turn your telemarketing into a successful part of your job hunting.

Preparing your action plan

This is part of your self-marketing campaign, in which you set out a plan of action so that you can achieve your objective. Try a little brainstorming here. Write down as many ideas as possible in about five minutes of the purpose of your calls, whom you will be calling, when and how they will be made and what kind of information you are looking for. All this can then be put on to a small database, with entries for such things as details of organisation, type of sector, contact names, addresses, titles, telephone numbers, faxes, e-mail. You may want to include details of current activities or performance, news gleaned from papers, journals, reports and networking contacts. Research in well-stocked and specialist commercial or university libraries for information on products or services, sector trends and industry developments. Competitors as well as your network contacts can often give valuable insights into current or future labour needs. You can also pick up information at trade fairs, conventions, conferences and promotional events. Try to grade all this information in some kind of 'prospect order'; is it very hopeful, might bring something, or just no use? Concentrate on those likely to bring a positive response, while being aware you may be strung along by organisations who are in no hurry to make a decision. Establish how many calls you will make, when they will be made, and then regularly check on the reaction you are receiving. If your approach meets with continual rejection or indifference, then your message and your questioning techniques need altering. While telemarketing may be seen by some selectors as irritating and putting them on the spot, if handled intelligently and tactfully it can be most useful in providing quality information on an organisation's needs and prospects.

Who are you going to speak to?

Reaching a key decision maker may prove difficult. Often they are screened by secretaries or they are on the move, with limited time to devote to unsolicited calls from prospective job hunters. While you may feel the more senior the person, the more influence they exert in taking people on, this may not always be the case. In flatter or more empowered organisations, hiring can be delegated downwards to line managers. Ascertain at an early stage, often by ringing in advance with a general enquiry, who is the best person to approach. Clarify that person's name, position, where located and the best time to make telephone contact. If a formal letter or CV is needed in advance of any discussion over the telephone, then comply with the request. Contact outside traditional hours of 9 to 5 may be a good way of reaching someone who has a hectic schedule and a crowded diary.

What are you going to say?

With only a few minutes to make a favourable impression, your aim is to quickly establish common ground with your contact. You will need to show there is a useful match between what you are conveying and what your contact feels or needs. Your opening remarks should indicate who you are and why you are calling. Set out in about one sentence what your overall aim is in making contact. Then give two or three brief indicators of the benefits you can bring and any special features of your skills and experience which are likely to be of special interest in solving problems. Have at the ready three or four structured questions which will help you to determine the needs of the organisation and its likely prospects. Consider any objections which may be fired at you and prepare some short replies. Throughout, listen carefully, be polite and positive and at the close create the opportunity to get in touch again if necessary. Even if the initial response is not encouraging, things may change and the prospect of ringing back in a few weeks may bring a more positive result. Your objective should be to give concrete examples of how you can provide quantifiable benefits, how you go about solving problems, and what you can introduce which is innovative and creative. Extract information from your personal dossier. Then go over your prepared script and amend it as you become more confident and assured in your approach.

How are you going to say it?

How you say things may well be more important than what you say in building up your mental image. Pay great care to your diction, your accent, your phrasing and your pitch and pattern of speech. If you rush your words, fail to enunciate clearly, pitch too high or low, demonstrate poor grammar and sentence construction, then your message loses its impact and meaning. Aim for a rate of about 150 words per minute. If your call is only four minutes, even without interruptions, you have about 600 words with which to persuade someone you are worth seeing. Keep your sentences brief, concise and avoid jargon and slang. You may find that standing up helps you to relax, while putting a smile in your voice conveys friendliness. Construct three or four versions of your 'mini-presentation', then work on it until you have one which gives the impression you are enthusiastic, articulate, confident and with something to offer which is of value and interest.

How can you monitor your performance?

In some respects, telemarketing yourself is somewhat of a numbers game. The more people you contact, the greater your chance of finding a rewarding opening. You will be attempting to stimulate interest in yourself as a source of value and potential benefit. To ensure you are making progress, establish performance indicators on a record card. List calls made and to whom, reaction to each call, leads established, appointments confirmed, follow-up procedures, information gleaned. If you run into a series of objections which may be difficult to deal with 'on the spur of the moment', make a note of them; then prepare a set of brief answers which effectively handle the objection. Establish what is your 'hit rate', in terms of the ratio of calls to appointments. Constantly work on your script, your means of establishing rapport, and your methods of projecting your personality over the telephone. Research shows that the mental image you leave behind will be the critical part of your telemarketing. Leave nothing to chance. Success will come largely through your meticulous attention to detail and your continual monitoring of the impact you are making.

RESPONDING TO ADVERTISEMENTS

If you rely on advertisements for your job hunting, it is highly probable you will become disillusioned with the response (or lack of it) you receive. Your route to success is far more likely to lie through your networking, or through specialist recruiters, as well as direct approaches to targeted organisations. This is not to say you should ignore advertisements. In some cases they can lead to an interesting and rewarding appointment. For example, the majority of public sector posts are still advertised but you will need to be aware that these may not always be as open as they seem. A likely candidate may already be under serious consideration.

Nevertheless, be realistic when considering advertised vacancies and approach them with some caution to avoid unnecessary disappointment. While recent figures indicate about 300,000 vacancies are now advertised, estimates suggest these account for only some 4 per cent of all jobs available. About 10 per cent of managers and professionals obtain their jobs through the appointments pages of quality newspapers. In terms of very senior appointments, about 15 per cent only of these are advertised, with the majority filled by firms using the specialised services of executive search consultants. By all means follow trends and developments in the appointments pages of good quality newspapers. You can scan these for indications of rewards packages and to gauge who is advertising and what they require of *an ideal candidate*. In certain cases you may feel you have seen 'the perfect job' and feel tempted to dash off your CV and covering letter.

While you may argue that someone has to be appointed, so why not you, let us look at advertised vacancies with a sense of realism. Here are three basic problems you will need to consider.

- Many job specifications are tightly drawn, to deter speculative applicants. If you cannot meet at least 85 per cent of what is required then you will normally receive a standard rejection. Behind a tight specification may lie even more stringent requirements, and you are unlikely to know much about these as an outsider.
- If the wording of the advertisement is vague and imprecise, then the response could well be overwhelming. Your

application will then receive very little attention and you may find you have been *over scanned*, even though you may be a good fit for the job.

- If you wish your application to remain confidential and not divulged to your current employer, then be especially aware of responding to box numbers. You could end up applying to your own firm!

Having said all that, here are some basic rules you should stick to when replying to advertisements:

- To avoid a pile of rejection letters, which often dampen your spirits, only respond when you can clearly establish you fit almost all of the specified criteria. Carefully dissect the advert, establishing what are the vital ingredients of the job and the person. Look hard at the 'key responsibilities' and the 'ideal requirements', as well as any specific qualifications required. Then endeavour to weigh these against what you can offer. If there are any gaps or reservations about your application, then do not expect to progress much further. Because advertised jobs have clearly entered the public domain, this makes them much more competitive. A sensible approach is for you to be highly selective and highly critical of your own suitability. This will enable you to keep your responses down to manageable proportions.

- Avoid sending a standard letter and CV. Instead, tailor both to the exact requirements of the job as advertised. Where possible, undertake research about the role and organisation. Keep your CV to two pages of A4 and ensure your one-page letter emphasises how well you meet the person and job requirements. Keep matters factual, start and end on a confident and positive note (eg I look forward to hearing from you ...). Post your application to arrive mid-week, and stick to the advice about the format of your CV contained in the next chapter.

- Look upon advertisements as a supplementary source, rather than your main method of job hunting. Become aware of extravagant claims like 'exceptional opportunities': 'outstanding benefits packages': 'great new window of opportunity'. Advertising hype may present a glowing picture but the reality may be very different. Devise a card to record precise details of each application. Retain a copy of the advertisement and if invited for a discussion, endeavour to find out as much as possible about the job, the organisation and the industry or sector beforehand. If the position is being handled by an agency or selection consultants, they may not wish to divulge too many details before an initial screening interview.

TIPS FOR YOUR FUTURE DEVELOPMENT

1. Look upon your job hunting as a game – not any old game but one where you play for high stakes. It's not like a game you have played before, because it's dynamic. The rules and players continually change. The right move brings rewards, the wrong move brings rejection.
2. Prepare to change positions and organisations more frequently in the future. Put a heavy emphasis on being up-to-date. Continually scan the horizon for prospects and opportunities.
3. View your job hunting as an intense and continual process of collecting detailed, high quality information about potential openings. The more you acquire, the greater your chances.
4. Thoroughly understand the market you are in. Define the needs and wants of your customers and how you can position yourself to satisfy these on a long term basis.
5. Being successful in your job hunting will depend heavily on your personality. The market favours those who are creative, resilient, conscientious and have sound inter-personal and team building skills.

Part Two:

Creating a Campaign which brings Results

3

Promoting Yourself and Persuading Others: What it Takes to Design and Develop Your CV

INTRODUCTION

In the last chapter we showed how your skills in planning, researching and marketing help you target different aspects of the job market. You have now reached the stage of *promoting yourself*. This is part of your overall marketing strategy and a important factor in your job hunting. If you are convinced you are a valuable and reliable asset to an organisation, emphasise it. Modesty will not be sufficient. In the future, your personal progression will require an even more persuasive attitude. You will therefore need to do two things here. First, sell yourself and your ideas in the best possible format. Secondly, overcome any reservations you may have on self-promotion or stage-managing your behaviour.

The reason for this is that the nature of the job hunting game has changed. Recruiters in all aspects of the job market now give much more weight to the different ways in which professionals and managers promote themselves and impress others with their worth and value. Not only is there a greater emphasis on communication and presentation skills. Just as important is your ability to stay visible, to develop ideas and to be creative and innovative. These issues apply if you are seeking continual career advancement in order to attain the upper reaches of your chosen field. They are just as important if you want to enhance your current role, even though for the time being you may be satisfied and comfortable within it.

In this chapter we will look at how you conduct your *self-promotion campaign*; in other words, organising your promotional literature to achieve a specific purpose. We aim to help you design, distribute and effectively communicate what you have to offer to your target market.

Building your campaign involves two important issues:

1. Awareness of what you are actually offering to potential employers. You can present this in various ways: for example, your skills, experience, potential, creativity, personality, problem-solving ability. You can give these different emphasis, depending on your range and depth of experience.

2. Determining what form your promotion should take, often referred to as your *promotional mix*: this can be broken down into the two main approaches favoured by job hunters, namely:

   ■ Your *curriculum vitae* (often abbreviated as CV and usually two pages in length) or your *resume* (popular in the USA and usually only one page in length).
   ■ Your *covering letters*.

Look upon these as *essential tools in successful job hunting*. When you have created both an appropriate CV and covering letter, then each should be evaluated against the check-list at the end of this chapter. By developing this approach you will be better equipped to assess the effectiveness of your promotional material. Nevertheless, your CV and covering letters are only part of your overall promotion campaign. We have already given some pointers to your *telemarketing* in the last chapter. You will also need to consider the importance of *networking*. This we treat separately in Chapter Five because of its special significance in bringing success in your job hunting.

Building an effective campaign is likely to combine all these tools at different stages and in different ways. All of them have a proven track record in enhancing your ability to confer benefits and satisfaction to potential employers. Nevertheless, if they are to work, you will have to finely tune and balance them so that the overall mix meets the specific needs of the different contacts you are targeting. *The aim of your marketing strategy is quite simple — offering the right blend of skills and experience at the right price, in the right location to satisfy an employer's expectations.*

YOUR CV AS A MARKETING TOOL

Traditional job search has always put a heavy emphasis on the importance of your CV and covering letter. This CV/resume-driven approach has been based on the premise that if you send plenty out and hope for the best, then something is likely to turn up. In the current climate of increased competition for all types of managerial and professional jobs, this is no longer a sound strategy to follow. A much more sensible approach, and one which is likely to bring positive results in the form of meetings and interviews, is to adopt the following:

1. *Be selective in your approach.* Ask yourself what motivates you to send your CV and covering letter to a prospective employer or recruiter. Is it your knowledge, attitude, experience, skills, credentials or personality which you feel equips you to meet the needs of the position? Have you undertaken a careful review of all those factors which an employer might take into account when filling the role? If so, compare and contrast these to see if there is a 'good fit' between what you can offer and what is realistically expected or required. If significant gaps or omissions occur, then there is little point in applying. Your aim is to target what is realistically feasible, not to back rank outsiders with no chance of success. Receiving a string of rejection letters

can be very disheartening and demotivating, and doesn't help you to reach the short-list.

2. *Research the market.* Here you need to find out what employers within specific sectors are looking for. Is it familiarity with the latest technology, experience in a particular industry, responsibility for a specialist function, or potential for future development? Construct your own list by reading quality newspapers, industry-specific journals, advertisements or by telephoning key people in the industry or profession, attending conferences and exhibitions. All of these will give you a much clearer idea of how to meet current needs and enable you to design your promotional material accordingly.

THE PURPOSE AND DESIGN OF YOUR CV

This can be considered under four main headings:

1. What is the purpose of your CV in the current job market?
2. What are the critical issues which you have to consider in its design?
3. How can you evaluate it to heighten its impact on the recipient?
4. To whom will you send it, along with your covering letter?

Essentially, the *purpose* of your CV is that of a self-marketing tool which portrays your skills, experience, achievements and potential for a specific objective. Its language creates meaning and interest in the mind of the recruiter. You use it to be invited to a meeting or short-listed for interview. Some writers regard this as its sole purpose. It puts you in front of decision makers but it doesn't guarantee a job offer. However, a CV does have other roles to play. It frequently forms the basis of an interview, where the interviewer will follow the format of your CV and ask you questions, often quite searching and penetrating ones, on what you have written. This is where the issues of credibility and verification really come into their own !

Be sure you can defend what you have written. Your CV can also form part of the basis for your contract of employment, especially if your future employer does not use standard application forms. In addition, your CV is a summary of relevant biodata on you and your employment history. It should also emphasise what you are capable of contributing now and what you wish to do in the future. It is your calling card to remind people who you are when you are not there yourself.

Several *critical design issues* also need to be considered. Strive to keep it to two pages (unless you have very extensive experience which you wish to set out in three pages). Have it laser printed on good quality A4 paper, preferably crisp white. Your first page should be very clearly set out, capable of grabbing attention and exciting interest. Avoid underlining or a mixture of font styles, be sparing in the use of italics, with plenty of white space to make it easier to scan. Resist the temptation to cram everything in. This makes it difficult to read and to convey meaning to what you are trying to portray. Your overall layout, grammar, spelling and punctuation should be beyond reproach.

In addition, your employment history should be in reverse chronological order, with far more emphasis on recent experience. Avoid sending photographs unless asked for; do not enclose testimonials or references, or copies of credentials and do not give salary details unless these are specifically requested. You should strive to think of your overall design within seven relevant sections, namely:

1. your personal details – who you are, where you can be contacted, date of birth, marital status
2. your education – in what institutions or settings and over what periods
3. your qualifications – what you have studied and learned and with what results
4. your career objective or profile – what you are seeking and for what reasons
5. your record of employment – who have you worked for and what have you achieved

6. your training and development – what enhances your marketability and competency
7. your additional data pertinent to the position – what else others may regard as important

In reviewing your final design, critically assess how far it is clear and easy to read, and how well it presents information which is relevant to the job or organisation you have in mind. Research findings consistently show that the format and overall appearance of the CV can be weighed as heavily as its content.

Now you reach the critical stage of *evaluating* your CV. Bear in mind that this will probably be read by people who will have no other insight into your personality, skills, experience or potential, other than what is laid out before them. Therefore a very useful tip here is to apply the *recruiter's* test to your efforts; namely how will a *potential buyer* of your services view you in terms of:

■ Do your stated job objectives match the position for which you are applying?
■ Does your CV match the precise criteria laid down for desired job performance? eg must have .... and ideally should be able to..............................
■ Are your accomplishments and identifiable skills easy to discern and do they fit what the recruiter is actually looking for?
■ Is it clear not only what you can do (eg credentials, languages, systems, marketing) but also how you will do these (such as meeting deadlines, negotiating under pressure, management style, interpersonal and leadership capabilities)?
■ Have you provided hard evidence of real accomplishments with quantifiable and verifiable results? For more senior positions, do you show a consistent growth of responsibility over a period of time?
■ Have you given an indication of your ability to relocate should this be necessary?

Who the likely *targets* of your CV are will largely depend on the nature and intensity of your job search. There are several options open to you:

- Responding to advertised vacancies; these can be placed through an agency, or search and selection consultants, or by the organisation concerned, or even through a box number.
- Sending direct to an agency or selection consultants; this may be unsolicited, or in response to their request to know more about you, or just to keep in touch on a regular basis.
- Targeting selected organisations which you have already researched and consider worth pursuing, either unsolicited, or again after an initial conversation and request for your CV.
- Mailing to your networking contacts who would welcome your approach and wish to help.
- Placing it on the Internet in one of a growing number of web sites which are now devoted to the distribution of CVs; you will need to be cautious here if confidentiality is important.

Each of these options can open up different prospects for you and you should attempt to use as many avenues as possible to exploit the opportunities which each one provides. In a sense, keeping all these options open is rather like a complex juggling act. Some will yield little return while others may produce the most unexpected results.

STANDARD TYPES OF CV

Some job hunters have taken to heart the frequent criticism of the boring, standard CV often produced by professional CV writers or outplacement firms. Some experienced recruiters even assert that they can actually identity the particular organisation which has produced a packaged format with standard layout, fonts, phraseology, profiles, achievements and job descriptions. To avoid being typecast, or to appear boring, the job hunter then goes in search of something different in order to appear distinctive. Eye catching type styles are used, paper is heavily coloured, text is surrounded with stunning graphics, photographs are incorporated, and ring binders are used to hold the finished product together. Unfortunately, appealing to the recruiters of professional and managerial positions by sending them something out of the ordinary is almost always bound to fail. If the organisation is already using automated CV tracking systems (the scannable CV referred to later in this chapter) then this kind of format will certainly not be acceptable.

Despite reservations about standardised CVs, and, as a job hunter you may have some genuine grounds for treating them with care, the essential fact is that there are established and recognised types or formats for your CV. These come under the headings of:

■ Chronological
■ Functional
■ Combination (of chronological and functional)
■ Electronically scannable

Using these to fit your own circumstances and individuality is a sensible way to start. It is likely to achieve the most success in securing what your CV really sets out to do – *to obtain an interview*. In considering how you should draft it to achieve its primary objective, endeavour to model your CV on what can be termed 'best practice in application form design'. Think carefully about *what* information is most likely to be needed by the reader, and *how* you will set this out to convey your message clearly and accurately. This is where standard types or formats can really help you to start the process, before you round off by stamping a little of your personal style on the finished work.

THE CHRONOLOGICAL CV

This moves back through time, giving greater attention to your most recent experience while at the same time showing increasing degrees of responsibility and variations in work environments. This type of CV enables you to demonstrate progress in your career and to highlight the extent of your specialisation and the skills you have used within each position. It also helps to indicate what you have accomplished within particular roles or environments. These can be highlighted in the form of achievements. These enable you to stand out from the competition. Employers often view high performers with special interest.

Given their importance in promoting yourself, how you establish and demonstrate your achievements becomes a vital part of your documentation. Here are three ideas you will find of value when drafting both your CV and covering letter.

1. Always consider the meaning of your achievements to your target-audience. Are you seen as someone who has done a sound job already and is capable of repeating it in a new setting? Do they show you can save time or improve profitability, or reduce costs while boosting production? Are they about solving problems, designing new systems, creating new openings or effective team playing? Endeavour to pick those parts of your performance which are likely to address the reader's concerns and at the same time benefit the goals of the organisation.

2. Show how your achievements came about by constructing a format which addresses three key questions. First, what was the problem you encountered or the challenge you had to meet? Secondly, how did you approach the problem/challenge and what particular technique(s) did you use to solve it? Thirdly, how did things work out in terms of results or measurable benefits? Remember, not all your endeavours will amount to success.

3. Focus on achievements which indicate particularly important skills within professional or managerial roles,

irrespective of whether you are starting out in your career or are already at a senior level. Your ability to build co-operative teams, to present ideas clearly, to form concepts or models, or to plan and structure a project within tight budgets and time limits, are all worthy of elaboration. If you have done something out of the ordinary in terms of project work, special assignments, creative thinking or research and development which sets you apart from the competition, then tell your reader about it.

Here are three examples of achievements which create a negative impact because they are too vague and imprecise. They fail to give any quantification, provide no real insight into what skills or competencies were used, or what benefits arose, or whether it was your work or that of others in the team.

1. Created controls and adaptations to facilitate the integration of a computerised system.
2. Set up financial, budgeting and monitoring systems for independent profit centres.
3. Established professional marketing, desk-top publishing and production functions.

Following this three-part approach (*problem – approach – outcome benefits*), here are three examples of achievements which give far greater insight into a candidate's performance.

1. Faced with 32 computer illiterate, under-performing middle managers, personally designed and delivered a computer familiarisation course, achieving a 95 per cent pass rate, increasing self-worth and motivation, leading to 30 per cent first year increase in departmental productivity in order processing and customer service.
2. Inheriting ineffective manual forecasting procedures, sourced, evaluated and successfully integrated a fully networked computerised package, based on weekly returns, leading to a saving of 20 per cent of staffing costs in first year (approx. £350K); now adopted as standard practice within the group.

3. Initially recruited to dispose of a loss-making subsidiary, subsequently revitalised existing management team by coaching, mentoring and training, resulting in a dramatic turn-round of motivation and performance, with £3.4M loss translated into £4.2M net profit within last two years.

Since most successful managers and professionals possess about three or four high performance competencies, then it is best to highlight these rather than attempt to give the mistaken impression that you are good at everything. You will also need to demonstrate, in any subsequent interview, how these are transferable and capable of raising the level of performance within your targeted organisation. Endeavour to group your particular achievements to fit your specialist area wherever possible. These may be in marketing, or logistics, finance or industrial relations, general or facilities management. They may also be in a specialised field within your particular profession such as employment law, coffer-dam construction, fraud investigation or financial restructuring. Two other points are worth considering before we leave the issue of achievements. Firstly, construct a set of action words which reflect the everyday language and terminology of your particular speciality. Then weave these into your CV and letters. Secondly, be aware of what employers are looking for when reviewing what you have achieved. They will be interested in you improving standards, eliminating waste, building a successful team, seizing opportunities or streamlining an operation.

Chronological formats are not only very common; they are also an important and convenient way of showing what you have achieved and experienced during a stable and progressive career. A brief scan identifies quality of credentials, level and range of experience, job and sector movement and the nature of your achievements. It can also show if your CV is too wordy, incomplete or hard to follow, all of which are bases for being bypassed. On page 72 we give an example of the front page of a *chronological CV*.

Rather than simply aping this format, you will achieve better results by using it as a basic template. Taking on board the advice we have just offered about layout and wording, you should try a number of versions until you convey the meaning you want to give to your target audience. However, this format is far less valuable if you have had numerous job changes, or perhaps false starts in different sectors, and where your performance has been variable or undistinguished. A probing interview is likely to highlight some of your performance deficiencies as well as raising doubts about your goals and commitment. In this case you would be well advised to consider the *functional CV* format which will enable you to focus more sharply on the skills you possess and prefer to use.

Sample Chronological CV emphasising performance

JOHN MARTIN RICHARDS

ORCHARD COTTAGE, DOWNING LANE, HARROGATE, HG3 5NP
TEL. NO. 01782 465310 (Home) 0321 48567 (Mobile)
e-mail rich@merlin.prestel.ac.uk

Date of Birth 24th March, 1963   Married, with two children
Education: Brasenose College, Oxford (Harper Scholar, 1981-84), The College of Law, London (1984-85)
Qualifications: B.A. in Law (First Class Hons) 1984, Admitted as Solicitor in 1987, MBA (LBS) 1994

EXPERIENCE PROFILE

A Principal Consultant and Senior Commercial Lawyer with ten years broad exposure in large commercial projects gained within two City practices and an international management consultancy. Currently managing a multi-disciplinary team with a personal operating budget of £200M, specialising in takeovers, mergers and acquisitions, MBOs, and flotations for a wide range of international clients. A demonstrable record of personal development and success in high level business negotiations, backed by in-depth knowledge of IT and emerging markets in the Far East. Recent achievements are:

■ Created and led a business development strategy, built on modern marketing techniques and sound financial models, leading to a doubling in consultancy fees over the past two years.
■ Personally developed a series of long-term contracts with key international clients, based on extensive customer analysis and innovative solutions, resulting in trebling of share in Far East market in last year.
■ Designed and managed a major two year programme of change in culture, systems and behaviour in an established but staid City practice; repositioning now generating higher revenues and service standards.

CAREER PROGRESSION

1994 to date	Global Management Consultants plc, Leeds	Principal Legal Consultant
1990–1994	Smith Bartram Hyde, Solicitors, Cheapside, London	Senior Commercial Lawyer
1987–1990	Clifford-Wren and Co. Solicitors, Chancery Lane, London	Commercial Solicitor
1984–1987	Simpson and Stroude, Solicitors, Kingsway, London	Articles, Assistant Solicitor

ADDITIONAL INFORMATION

Primary school Governor. Currently studying Mandarin Chinese. Fluent in French. Advanced Computer skills

To help you develop your own chronological CV from 'a standing start', here is an outline plan which you use as a form of check-list or guide to what is needed.

1. At the top of the page give your full name, preferably in bold capitals with spacing. Aim for a maximum 15–18 pt size.

2. Full address including post code, preferably on one line in smaller type 11/12 pt. If you are likely to move, include another contact address where you can be reached.

3. Telephone no. including other contact forms including mobile, fax or e-mail address; in 10/12 pt.

4. Date of birth (if omitted it tends to irritate and may lead to rejection). Marital status (if preferred).

5. Other information such as nationality, driving licence, can be included if relevant to the position. Keep this basic information in a tidy format, ensure it is well spaced and easy to read, with a single typeface using business-like fonts (eg Switzerland, Arial, Times New Roman) and justification on both sides. Avoid fancy font styles, underlining and over use of bold or italics. Boxes and shading should be used with care. Leave a space before the next part.

6. Here you have the option to include one of three important aspects of your *biodata*. It can be your education and training; or your overall career or job objective; or it can be your personal profile/experience summary. Much will depend on what you wish to emphasise and its importance in relation to the job or organisation you have in mind. If you are just starting out on the first rung of your professional or managerial career after completion of education or training, then your experience will be far less significant and you will be judged more on your credentials and future potential, and the clarity of your career or job objective.

Where you are seeking a more senior position, then your experience, embedded within your personal profile, is likely to be a better method of self-presentation. Let us look at each of these to see how they can be used to advance your suitability.

Education and Training – here you can include secondary schools, universities or colleges. Degrees, diplomas, certificates and other special qualifications, with dates and details, should be given, including specialist skills and languages, and selected training courses attended. Each one of these should be relevant and verifiable; set them out concisely and without ambiguity.

Overall career or job objective – this can be in the form of a two or three line statement in which you set out what you want to do or are qualified to do. For example, you may wish to stipulate the kind of position you are seeking or its level in the organisation. Again, you may indicate the type of organisation you have in mind (public sector, professional firm, consultancy) as well as its prevailing culture. In addition, you may wish to emphasise your skills and qualifications and how you wish to use these in your work. Such an objective not only indicates your interests and where you could slot into the organisation, it also gives a view of you as someone with skills and a sense of direction. You have the choice to make it narrow and specific or general, in which case it may convey no real meaning. Strive to make your statement realistic, especially if you are just beginning your career after graduation or training. Finally, gear it to the needs of the organisation or you risk being rejected. If you have a choice of different career directions, you can then create several versions of your objective statement.

Personal profile/experience summary – this is your opportunity to set out the important issues relating to your experience (depth, variety, transferability, relevance) and how these can be of benefit to the targeted organisation. Essentially this is in the form of an impact statement, where you are endeavouring to quantify your achievements, using action verbs which establish the value of your performance (eg reversed, directly negotiated, designed). If you are responding to an advertisement then you may wish to reiterate what is required in the job eg

*an energetic, performance driven MBA and Chartered Accountant
with direct responsibility for operating budgets of £230 million;
extensive change management experience within diverse service
organisations.*

Avoid using flowery or inflated descriptions of your
responsibilities. Instead, attract attention with the judicious
use of two or three bullet-pointed phrases, rather than relying
totally on narrative skills. Approach your drafting of a personal
profile with care to avoid being typecast as someone who may
be relying on the marketing skills of an outplacement
consultant rather than using your own phraseology. Try to
tailor your language to fit the prevailing culture of the targeted
organisation, and keep the overall length to about ten lines.

You now come to the part where you will be setting out
your career progression, usually in the form of a concise
history (dates, names of organisations and location, job title).
These will be in chronological order with the current or most
recent job first. Depending on how much material you already
have placed on your first page, you will then need to determine
how much of your experience you will divulge here rather than
leaving this to appear on your second page. Surveys indicate
that on average a recruiter's first scan of a CV takes 30 seconds,
and 80 per cent of this time is devoted to the first page. If you
do not have much space, and you have already put significant
emphasis in your profile or experience summary, then you
need to be brief and succinct eg

1993–to date	National Building Society Leeds	Divisional Manager
1990–1993	General and Mutual Brokers, Bristol	Deputy Divisional Manager

You will readily appreciate that much of this is basic
information set out in a chronological style. However, within
it there is significant *biodata* which is often regarded as an
important pointer to your future performance. Before leaving
page one, you will need to decide whether you wish to use
this purely as a resume, or whether you will now add 'flesh to
the bare bones' by elaborating upon your experience and
achievements, Adding a second page will give you the

opportunity to expand into areas which will give the recruiter a far greater insight into what you have to offer. Assuming you have carefully evaluated the strength of the message you wish to communicate on page one, then the format within the chronological CV remains the same. Your recent experience comes first, highlighting what is especially pertinent while not overplaying your hand. At the top of the second page, provide details of your current or most recent role. Following the earlier example you would elaborate as follows:

1993 to date	National Building Society, Head Office, Park Row, Leeds	Divisional Manager

Begin by indicating some of the key features of the organisation, eg turnover, number of employees, profitability, size, ownership, position within sector, current structure, scale of operations. This gives meaning to the setting in which you are currently operating. Then indicate where you fit within the structure, what you are responsible for and to whom, and what results you have produced over a period of time.

Keep these issues factual and avoid glamorising or overplaying your importance. You can then display several forms of achievement arising from your activities, preferably in the form of bullet-points. Ensure these are concise and contain quantifiable data, for example:

■ Selected, negotiated and implemented £3.4M management information system on time, within budget, leading to improved operating margins of 23 per cent and cost savings of £350K, over past two years

Do not give too many achievements since you may find you have fired all your best shots at once and have nothing in reserve for the interview. As a rough guide, do not exceed four for the position you wish to highlight most and for others stick to two or three. Jobs held over ten years ago should receive a one line treatment to be concise. Towards the foot of the page you could also indicate other factors which may be pertinent. These could include membership of professional bodies; methods of continuous professional development; outside voluntary or charitable work or awards which support your application and demonstrate your transferable skills; flexibility to relocate; additional assignments, not part of your job and outside normal hours, which produced positive benefits for yourself or your organisation. You may wish to indicate your availability to take up a position. If you are currently redundant, this could be immediately.

THE FUNCTIONAL CV/RESUME

Your format here will be rather different from that of the chronological CV. The approach changes to one where you are giving far greater emphasis to your key skills and potential. At the same time you are also de-emphasising your lack of experience or gaps in your employment history. Skills are specific areas of competence and qualifications where you have the confidence and ability to make a significant contribution without requiring additional training or practice. These can come under several headings such as:

Technical skills and professional qualifications – examples such as law, engineering, data processing, systems design, finance, marketing, logistics, computing.

Social and interpersonal skills – examples such as motivating and leading, patience, openness, conflict resolution, negotiating and presenting, persuading and team building.

Personal skills and reputation – examples such as creativity, conscientiousness, independence, maturity, charisma, flexibility, dependability, presence and charm, innovation, drive and confidence.

Managerial and communication skills – organising, planning, scheduling, co-ordinating, problem solving, supervising, mentoring, speaking, presentations, writing, foreign languages.

An example of the first page of a *functional CV* is given opposite. As a marketing tool, it does have several advantages eg:

■ When you are emphasising skills and capabilities which were not utilised to their fullest extent during your recent work experience (eg taking a temporary or stop-gap position).

■ When your work has been spasmodic or disrupted and you cannot demonstrate progressive career development or regular promotions.

■ When you wish to change career direction or are re-entering the labour market after a break such as extended redundancy, illness or bringing up a family.

■ When you have various but unrelated sets of work experiences in which you wish to focus on your overall personal qualities (adaptability, rapid learning ability, getting on with people).

Nevertheless, there is strong evidence that employers tend to view functional CVs rather more critically. In particular, they are likely to demonstrate a lack of experience, they do not show consistent career progression within a role or sector and they give scant attention to job titles and the nature of the actual job within the organisational structure. They are also far less common than their chronological counterparts and require far more effort on your part if you are to tailor them to show exactly what benefits you can bring to an organisation.

Sample Functional CV

MARGARET JANE PICKERING
27, MAYCROFT AVENUE, FLITTERTON, OXFORDSHIRE, OX9 5PZ – 01869 009444

CAREER OBJECTIVE	A demanding position within an innovative and dynamic Marketing Department which will enable me to effectively utilise my sales, commercial, linguistic and computer skills to enhance departmental performance and raise its profile within the Company
EXPERIENCE SUMMARY	Eleven years post-graduate experience in responsible and progressive roles in international sales, marketing and financial services. Currently managing a sales force of 75 operating out of seven branch offices for a major financial services group
SALES	Developed and managed key accounts in three diverse industries (publishing, food, and financial services). Consistent record of sales growth and profits margins. Designed new sales training modules leading to 24 per cent increase in field sales over two years
COMMERCIAL	Initial role of Assistant to Marketing Director of prestigious publishing house, followed by four years developing European food sales for international brand leader. Main responsibilities involved customer service, budgeting, forecasting, database marketing
LANGUAGE AND COMPUTER SKILLS	Fluency in French and Spanish obtained as graduate and enhanced during international travel on sales assignments and training of field staff. Proficiency in W4W, Excel, Powerpoint. Responsible for sourcing and delivery of multi-media distance learning packages to field staff in £13M sales operation
WORK EXPERIENCE 1995 to date	FINANCIAL SERVICES CORPORATION Global Financial Services with Washington HQ Field Sales Manager
1991–1995	FOOD BRANDS PLC European distributor of high quality fresh produce Training Coordinator, Training Manager, then Senior Training Manager
1986–1991	ORIENT PUBLISHERS PLC Speciality publishers of scientific and technical books Marketing Assistant, Area Sales Representative, then Assistant Marketing Manager
EDUCATION	BA Hons. in Business Studies & Modern Langs. (Upper Second) Aston Univ. 1986 Member of Chartered Institute of Marketing 1993
PERSONAL	Date of Birth 12 July 1965 Single British Nationality

THE COMBINATION CV

Essentially, this is where you are endeavouring to combine the different styles and benefits which can be derived from both chronological and functional formats. The *combination CV* is especially valuable when you wish to demonstrate that:

■ You have behind you a track record of solid performance and progression which shows success.
■ There is nothing you would wish to de-emphasise such as false starts, gaps, redundancy, dismissal.

Within a combination CV you will need to pay particular attention to the following:

Your career summary or profile – this should be expanded upon to show how your range of skills and personality traits have, for example, enhanced productivity and produced demonstrable results, or have brought a turnaround in fortunes, or they have brought a change in corporate culture. It should also focus on your potential and where you envisage your next role to be. This is your opportunity to engage carefully in self-promotion by conveying your abilities and accomplishments.

Your functional skills – here you will be emphasising your range of functional skills while showing how these contributed to performance through different achievements. You will need to tailor these to the position you have in mind, especially if it is in response to a tightly worded advertisement.

Your concise career history or employment record – often placed towards the foot of page one, when you revert to a chronological format, showing organisations with dates, titles and an indication of your steady progression within a sector or professional role.

An example of a *combination CV* is given opposite.

Sample combination CV

MICHAEL ROYSTON FIELDING

88, LANCHESTER ROAD, QUEENSWAY, LONDON, WC3 4QP
Tel. No. 0171 385 012220   Mobile 0734 464646

OBJECTIVE

Human Resources Director

SUMMARY	Eighteen years of lecturing, training and human resource management experience in responsible positions in universities, telecommunications and pharmaceuticals markets
UNIVERSITY LECTURING	Responsible for the development and marketing of post-graduate HRD courses at MBA and MSc level in two major Business Schools. Achieved over 200 per cent growth in admissions over three years, leading to top grade performance rating and awards
TRAINING AND DEVELOPMENT	Recruited, trained and managed wide variety of teams in multi-site operations using up-to-date interviewing, testing, counselling and performance appraisal techniques. Standardised selection methods produced higher productivity and lower turnover
HUMAN RESOURCE MANAGEMENT	Revitalised an underperforming pharmaceuticals business by complete change of recruitment and selection methods, driving through an empowerment culture and developing quality initiatives. Savings of £1.2M achieved on manpower budget
EXPERIENCE	BIOTECH PHARMACEUTICALS PLC. 1993 to date Speciality Biotechnology and Over the Counter Drugs Firm Personnel Manager 1993–95, Senior Personnel Manager 1995

Key responsibilities include:

- Managing team of 32 professionals providing full range of HRD services to Board and line managers; redesign of all recruitment policies over last two years
- Design and delivery of corporate culture change strategy reporting to main Board
- Leading corporate team charged with redefining and improving quality standards to meet latest EC regulations

You can continue this chronological format on page two, incorporating responsibilities and achievements, and then placing details of education, qualifications and training, along with date of birth etc at the bottom of the page. By mixing both functional and chronological styles, you can thus produce different designs.

THE ELECTRONICALLY SCANNABLE CV – WHAT IT MEANS FOR YOU

This type of CV represents a significant departure from the conventional CVs which we have just been discussing. Essentially, the scannable CV is designed to be entered into a computerised database using an optical scanner. A scanner is a device which captures an image (it could be text, drawing, photograph, or even a relatively flat object like your hand). Your CV, however it arrives (e-mail, fax, letterpost) will first be scanned into a computer as an image, not text, by means of OCR (optical character recognition) software. This examines the image to distinguish every letter and number and then creates a text file (ASCII) which the computer is able to understand. Once your CV is in computer-readable format, it can then be stored within different forms of software, eg databases, spreadsheets, word processors, desktop publishers. When asked to, computer software can screen or identify qualified candidates on the basis of *a search of key words or phrases*. These can be your name, age, address, qualifications, type of experience, work history, level of responsibility, and skills. This varied information can then be collected and stored in CV format or even condensed into a professional profile or summary.

Having stored all the CVs received in response to an advert, or those which arrive unsolicited, a recruiter can then quickly stipulate the specific requirements for the ideal candidate. In some cases, these may be far more restrictive than emphasised in the advertisement. These are often couched in general terms to attract a very wide variety of applicants. A key word search is made within the database (eg find me someone 25 to 40, living within a 20 mile radius, with an MBA and marketing experience in the food industry). By changing and adjusting the criteria, a recruiter will normally be able to find a manageable number of applicants who fit the job specification and who can be invited for interview.

These developments in document imaging technology will mean your CV will increasingly be stored in electronic format, able to be indexed and retrieved very rapidly, even on a remote access basis. Tracking and identifying suitable candidates for current and future jobs will be just like identifying orders, invoices or accounts. It is these technology-driven changes which are rapidly replacing paper-based searches for suitable candidates, especially at the initial or screening stage. In future, these recruitment systems are highly likely to make the advice about creating the perfect CV either superfluous or obsolete. For the recruiter it will bring faster and more accurate scanning of suitable applicants. Indeed, as skills shortages for certain knowledge workers continue to cause problems for recruiters, a number of expanding organisations are now recognising the value of actively encouraging candidates to submit CVs for future consideration. These are then frequently reviewed to see if there is an appropriate match with any current or future vacancy.

Given these developments, it is important that you invest time and effort to focus on two main issues, namely what they signify for you as a 'job hunter', and what you need to do to adapt to these requirements. First, recruiters and employers will increasingly use software which scans rather than reads the key words and phrases which they feel summarise the important characteristics sought in applicants for a particular position. Here are six examples taken from advertised vacancies which emphasise such factors as age, qualifications and level of experience. You will notice that each one demands a very tight set of criteria. Applicants outside these limits may experience difficulty in being considered for interview.

- Aged 25–40, MBA essential, currently working for major international blue chip in the electronics industry and with hands-on experience of selling software solutions to major clients.
- 35 +, good degree in food science, with minimum of five years cross-functional project management experience in a major food manufacturer.
- Practical skills in business process re-engineering or strategic IS planning along with a minimum of four years consulting experience at international level.
- Young ACA, must be 'big six' trained, minimum of two years management accounting in a multi-media environment; must possess high degree of computer literacy.
- Mid 30s graduate in business management, fluent in French and Spanish, and with direct marketing experience of branded consumer pharmaceuticals in African markets.
- PhD, at least three years experience working with derivatives products, strong computing and mathematical skills, fluency in Turkish, English and another European language.

Each of these examples contain key words or phrases regarded as prerequisites of successful job performance.

If you were to apply for any one of the six examples above, a scanner would process your CV in a few seconds and if, after a key word search, you did not meet the predetermined criteria, then a tracking system would normally generate a rejection letter. In the case of unsolicited CVs, then these can be electronically stored and reviewed to see if there is an appropriate match with any current or future vacancy.

For you as a job hunter this will mean less reliance on subjective assessment by a recruiter. At the same time it will enable you to construct a CV which will stand a greater chance of success if it contains skills and other key words which match what the computer is searching for. However it will also mean your CV will have to be in a format and style which the scanner can read. Here are *four tips* to help you to meet the requirements of these technology-driven changes. By following these simple guidelines you will increase your chances of success.

1. *Your layout* – this should be left justified throughout; avoid fonts which are large, ornate and difficult to scan. Stick to standard sans serif ones such as Switzerland, Arial, Helvetica, which are very easy to read. Keep sizes within 10 to 14 points throughout. Using italics and resorting to heavy underlining tends to cause scanning problems, as will the use of shading and fancy graphics. Avoid these, along with brackets, compressed print, boxes, columns, pictures, double spacing and underlining. Use bold face for any emphasis needed (say for name of employer or position held) but try not to overdo this. Fancy, decorative formats slow down the scanning process and may distort the stored data. In a nutshell, keep it plain and simple, since the computer is reading text and not graphics.

2. *Your format* – you can use any standard CV format provided it is clean, clear and easy to read. The computer will be able to extract skills and other key words from the different formats we have identified such as chronological (where you list your jobs in reverse chronological order), or functional (where you focus on skills), or even combination CVs. You should use typical headings (in capitals) found in all CVs such as: Experience, Career History, Achievements, Skills, Education, Training, Qualifications, Publications, Professional Development, Summary of Accomplishments, Personal Strengths, etc. Ensure your name is at the top of the page, with address and phone details below.

3. *Use of White Space and Language* – Always aim for plenty of white space on your CV, particularly between the different sections we have discussed. It is easier to scan and easier to read. Ensure your paper is high quality, standard A4 size, crisp white and laser printed. This will enable your CV to present a clean image to the scanner. Do not send it by fax, which can distort; put your name, flush left at the top of each numbered page. Use paper clips: do not fold or

staple. Ensure you eliminate all personal pronouns such as me, my, I. Try to use key nouns in functional areas rather than too many action verbs or glorifying adjectives, such as directed, instigated, improved; avoid vague descriptions.

4. *Use of Key Words* – These come in various forms, but are related to skills, abilities and facts, such as your education, qualifications, knowledge and professional development. They are often regarded as descriptors or buzzwords and are the words or phrases which selectors search for when selecting candidates for shortlisting. They are a vital part of your scannable CV because you will rely on these to ensure you achieve as many 'hits' as possible. A 'hit' is when the computer, in its database search for specific key words or phrases, finds them in your CV. Thus, the more key word marketing points you can provide (ie credentials, skills) the greater your chances of being selected for interview from an electronic database. Therefore, become highly familiar with the use of *effective key words* or common language, in your specialist area by reviewing quality advertisements, consulting with professional re-cruiters, and keeping abreast of technical language. Instead, use concrete words or acronyms such as project manager, systems analyst, marketing, accountant, MBA, Unix. Technical phrases may also be used such as budget time frames; designing re-engineering solutions; developing interfaces from host systems; brown field engineering; project management; variable run lengths; mechanical fabrication and assembly systems. In addition, industry-standard terms, for example enhancing competitive advantage; implementing a systems strategy; developing a total quality initiative; revitalising the corporate culture; are frequently used. You may also wish to insert a keyword paragraph near the top of your first page, in which you list the keywords which indicate your transferable skills, qualifications and experience.

YOUR COVERING LETTER

If your CV is to be considered as one half of your marketing literature, then your covering letter is the other half and merits just as much attention and careful consideration. Alongside your CV, your covering letter is your attempt to control and influence the impressions which the reader will form when it is either scanned or carefully digested. Your aim here is to try to ensure you receive a positive response to your initial contact; *'yes, we would be most interested in seeing you to discuss how far you may be of benefit to our organisation...'.*

You can only do this if you go out of your way to present an image and to create a vital first impression of someone who is clearly worthy of further consideration. Two general issues arise here.

1. Ensuring that what you write reduces negative expectations — you can do this in various ways; by carefully checking such basic but frequently overlooked issues as spelling, grammar, punctuation, literary style, layout, typeface, length, conciseness, clarity of expression, paper quality and crispness of printing. Disregard these and your rejection letter will be on its way.

2. Conversely, ensuring that what you write enhances positive expectations — you can help here by undertaking research to find out what your target organisation actually needs and then communicating your ability to meet these needs (eg possessing a high level of general competence, specific transferable skills, meeting performance targets, displaying creativity and self-development). You can also endeavour to please your potential audience (eg in response to an advertised vacancy, or to a network contact) by positively enhancing your strengths while being careful not to exaggerate your accomplishments.

If you intend to convince the reader of your letter that you are worthy of serious consideration then you have to actively say so. Little may be achieved if you act modestly or fail to promote yourself and your track record. When you can quite legitimately claim personal responsibility for an event with a very positive and measurable outcome (eg improving customer service, designing innovative software, improving market share) then say so, or the opportunity to impress someone of your worth and potential may soon disappear. Until someone decides you are worth seeing, your paperwork, however it is presented, is all they have by which to judge you.

Before we turn to what you intend to *cover* in your accompanying letter, let us remind ourselves of some of the more general issues relating to the drafting of covering letters. Research findings indicate you need to take three important steps if you are to create a favourable impression.

1. Pay very careful attention to the *appearance* of your letter. Recruiters will expect you to produce it on one page of A4 size high quality white paper, laser printed, with rigorous attention paid to the production of a standard business letter. Forms of address, spacing, font style and use of reference numbers should follow normal business protocol. Make your finished product look professional and balanced; keep your message succinct and relevant. Don't cram the page with too much detail and, as with the CV, the use of white space is important.

2. Ensure that it has a defined *structure*. Where possible, address your letter to a specific person rather than a department such as personnel or marketing, and check you have the correct addressee details. Your opening paragraph should say why you are writing (eg responding to an advert, networking, direct mail shot to a targeted organisation) and demonstrate you have something of value to offer as well as showing you have done some background research. Then come right to the point in the main body of the letter. Cover your experience and achievements in no more than three paragraphs, carefully using bullet points to emphasise salient points. Conclude with a brief 'action' paragraph indicating your wish to discuss your application in more detail and that you will

telephone to see when an appointment can be made. In total try to limit yourself to 15–18 lines.

3. Endeavour to make the *content* interesting, relevant and imaginative wherever possible. It may not always be possible to make your letter fun to read, but try to give it a little sparkle. So many letters which reach recruiters are boring, tedious and dull. If you can convey a little of your own personality or enthusiasm and drive, then go for it!

Bearing these in mind, now think about some of the issues which you may wish to cover in your letter. Here are a selection:

■ You may wish to show the specific match or fit between what the job requires and what you can provide. This is important when answering advertisements and you could structure your response into two columns; on the left *what are you looking for* and on right *what I am able to offer*.

■ You may wish to highlight your particular qualifications and specialised training and their relevance within a particular targeted organisation, eg being up to date; at the leading edge; high quality; highly specialised; from a prestigious institution. This applies especially when you are starting out on your professional or managerial career and have relatively little experience but plenty of potential to offer.

■ You may wish to demonstrate your wide ranging and extensive experience and how this can be translated into specific and tangible benefits for the targeted organisation. Here your skills and achievements are given substantial coverage, indicating their transferability and versatility. Managerial and professional competencies become your key portable assets.

■ You may wish to centre upon some of your personality traits and how these can be used to good effect. While it is often difficult to be objective when engaged in self-reporting (*I am very good in a crisis. . .*) you can nevertheless stress your degree of commitment, level of conscientiousness, maturity, toughness to withstand pressure, dependability or level of energy. Indeed, many advertisements now specify a wide range of desired traits to accompany both skills and experience. Compile a list of these to see how they fit your own personality.

You may find it useful to build up a glossary of terms, phrases or paragraphs gleaned from adverts, personal contacts or letters you have seen, which can be used to good effect at a later date. Try to develop these so that they appear spontaneous and natural rather than contrived and false.

FALSEHOODS AND INACCURACIES IN THE CV

Recent surveys in the UK and the USA have shown a significant increase in the number of applicants falsifying their CV/resume in some way. In certain areas, particularly for more senior positions, up to one-third of CVs contain false information. This trend has arisen in response to the intense competition surrounding many positions and where applicants are endeavouring to impress by giving misleading or inaccurate information concerning a wide range of key issues. These include:

Qualifications — Claiming degrees and professional recognition which do not exist; universities and colleges which have not been attended; inflating degree performance; indicating courses which have not been studied or over-emphasising their importance.

Skills — False claims relating to language proficiency, computer knowledge, writing and speaking skills, operating procedures, scheduling and supervisory skills.

Experience — Falsely claiming the level, depth, extent and quality of experience; fake references.

Employment history — Inaccurate information relating to dates of appointment, location of work, type of industry or organisation; inventing grandiose job titles; inflating salaries and remuneration packages; hiding gaps in employment with fictitious employers; ambiguous reasons for leaving jobs.

These are clearly worrying and disturbing issues for those who receive CVs. Such a trend may well come to signify that as a marketing document the CV will be seen as less reliable and valid in content due to the level of falsification. For the job hunter the message is quite plain. Ensure that everything you write is true, accurate and capable of verification. Interviews are the occasion when your claims may well be very carefully scrutinised; you will be required to defend what you have written and any impression given that all is not what it seems will soon invalidate your application. Worse still, if at a later date an employer finds you have provided false information, a serious breach of contract could arise, leading to summary dismissal and even legal proceedings.

THE LIMITATIONS OF THE CV

It is somewhat illusory to think you can create an ideal or perfect CV even though it is an essential part of your overall marketing strategy. Just as there is no single best way to draft an advert, prepare a job description or conduct an interview, so this principle applies to your efforts to construct a one or two-page historical portrait of yourself as a valuable resource. A key issue to bear in mind is that many employers focus not on what you have done in the past, but what you can do for them in the future. Too many guides to CV writing assume that by following certain rules or formats, you as a job hunter will be able to meet with success. This is often far from the case. What you need to appreciate is that there is no right structure, format or design, simply because each person's perception of what is important in a CV will clearly differ. Some will always prefer a chronological approach while others will warm to a combination format or even welcome a purely functional one.

Your aim in all this is to direct your efforts specifically towards constructing a document which will fit as far as possible the jobs for which you wish to be considered as a serious applicant. Your CV is simply the *route to the interview, not the job itself.*

Let us now examine some of the distinct limitations of the CV within the job search process. These can be considered as follows:

- For many advertised vacancies, CVs have a notoriously low hit rate; it may well be less than 1 per cent simply because so many of them are very badly drafted, fail to meet the stringent criteria laid down and have not been adapted to meet the needs of the employer. Despatching large numbers of identical CVs for very different jobs is simply a waste of time, effort and valuable resources.
- The CV is only capable of conveying certain kinds of information. While you may feel you are able to match what has been stipulated in an advert, do bear in mind that it is the employer or selector who establishes the actual criteria. It is only by careful research into an organisation's needs or by understanding the recruiter's brief that you will be able to attract their interest and attention. In many instances, what you may feel you have to offer may only be of marginal importance and a hidden agenda may well apply.
- CVs which are not subjected to computer scanning are invariably rapidly scanned by the human eye, especially at the first stage of the sifting process. Estimates of the average time taken to scan vary between twenty and forty seconds. In this period selectors are very rapidly endeavouring to fit what you are presenting into their perception of some kind of ideal candidate.

Throughout this chapter the emphasis has been upon the effective preparation of your marketing literature, namely your CV and your covering letter. Various tips and ideas have been presented to you in the hope that they will give you a competitive edge in your job search activities. Nevertheless, these are only supporting tools within an overall strategy. In addition you will also need to incorporate such vital elements as interview skills, networking, negotiation and presentational skills while at the same time enhancing your future employability. All these are covered in detail in the remainder of this book.

A CHECK LIST OF YOUR PROMOTIONAL MATERIAL

- Is what you write short and simple, clear and concise?
- Are you consulting trade and professional journals along with current adverts to obtain a feel for the language in a specific sector?
- Are you able to turn dull and dry information into interesting and influential messages?
- Are you using a good dictionary and thesaurus to expand your word development?
- Have you avoided using flowery phrases and words which are vague and non-specific such as liaised, administered, co-ordinated; have you eliminated all the padding and verbosity?
- Are you able to convert technical language into understandable material for the non-expert reader?
- Have you paid very careful attention to your layout, drafting, grammar, spelling, punctuation and literary style – do you know these are the most common reasons for rejection by recruiters?
- Does your literature give a strong, credible indication of the range of problems you have met, the solutions you have applied and how these can help an employer?
- Are you carefully emphasising the results you have produced rather than compiling a dreary list of responsibilities, which may fail to indicate your success within each job?

4

The Art of Impression Management: Acting and Appearing Right for the Job

YOUR IMAGE AND IMPRESSION MANAGEMENT

Image is rapidly becoming a critical issue in successful job search. If you are to compete effectively in the future, then you will need to devote considerable attention to creating and developing *your total corporate image*. Your image is dictated by a simple ratio; two thirds of its impact will come from your non-verbal behaviour and only one third from your verbal behaviour. In this chapter we will focus on ways to help you project the right corporate image through your overall impression management. By so doing we aim to improve your own personal marketability.

Impression management relates to the different behaviours we display when we try to create and maintain a particular impression of ourselves. As an illustration, ask yourself how much do you reveal of yourself when you meet someone for the first time. What is it that you wish to disclose about yourself and is it the same or different from how others see you? For example, others may see you as reserved and cautious while you feel you convey an image of being lively and enthusiastic. In this case there is a clear gap between what you intend and what is actually perceived. Your ability to disclose aspects of yourself will largely depend on the situation in which you find yourself. You may find it easier to disclose far more to a close friend than a complete stranger. Yet there will be occasions in your job search when you will be asked to reveal a considerable amount of information about yourself to complete strangers, often in a short space of time. This applies in several situations: for example:

- while networking or information seeking — strangers will want to know about your accomplishments, career aims, future plans, track record of successes and failures, personality traits, hopes and fears;
- within the employment interview — strangers will again press you on achievements and disappointments, on skills and professional development, on your personal qualities and behaviour;
- during psychometric testing or within assessment and development centres — strangers will pose difficult and probing questions about your background, interests, managerial experience and leadership potential, stress resistance and creativity.

How much to reveal in such encounters may present you with a real dilemma. Hold back and you could be seen as reserved, withdrawn and suspicious. Reveal too much and you may be regarded as indiscreet, over confident and even embarrassing. In order to present yourself in the best light to others, some kind of balance has to be struck, depending on the preferences of your audience and how much you wish to volunteer about yourself. You may feel that modesty is important. You then understate your assets and achievements and give the impression that you are lacking in self-confidence. Overstate your case and you could be accused of bragging and boasting.

CONVEYING THE RIGHT IMPRESSION

Much of what you will do during your job search will involve a conscious attempt to manage the impressions you make on other people. Think again of the main opportunities you have to do this and also how far these will be effective and influential in achieving your objectives.

- ■ Your CV and covering letters – do these meet the criteria and expectations of recruiters?
- ■ Your networking and telemarketing skills – do these enable you to influence key decision makers?
- ■ Your interview techniques – are you presenting yourself in a favourable and desired image?
- ■ Your presentation abilities – are you enhancing your claims and making yourself attractive to others?

These are some of the tools and techniques which enable you to influence, as well as monitor, *two important aspects of your job hunting performance.*

First, analysing how far these tools and techniques influence the perception of others about you. In other words, do they enable you to look good to someone else whose support you are seeking.

Secondly, discovering how effective are the different approaches you use in projecting your own self-image. For managers and professionals, developing and maintaining a positive self-image, such as being friendly and hard-working, is a vital part of their work activity as well as their future employability.

It is relatively easy to recognise the importance of these different tools and techniques within job search. Indeed, a substantial proportion of job seekers will use most or all of them in different ways and with varying results. However, when these fail to achieve their objective and you end up disappointed and disillusioned, then you are likely to blame the very approaches which, if used effectively, can bring success. The difficulty lies in finding out what is required of each approach within each particular situation: then developing each one so that you perform well. Inevitably, this will depend on the resources you have to draw upon, especially in terms of your impression management behaviours and techniques.

You will need to quickly recognise the social situation in which you find yourself. Consider the audience you are addressing, and what rules of behaviour should apply. Within social encounters such as networking, interviews or making presentations, you are presenting yourself in two main forms. This will be mainly through your *verbal and non-verbal behaviour*. It will also come through your *appearance, clothes and forms of dress*. By using both formats, you will be projecting yourself on your audience.

However, the means by which you project yourself will also be monitored and evaluated, with people forming different impressions of you in the same way that you are forming impressions of them.

Let us now look at an important distinction in the way you convey impressions to others; namely how you choose to *appear* and how you choose to *act*.

How you choose to appear will be reflected partly in your dress. This can convey a great deal about your personality and the effort you are making to build your corporate image. By dressing professionally, you increase your chances of being more favourably evaluated. If you look the part and comply with the dress code of your chosen field, you are conveying to your audience the impression of reliability and discretion. Your personal appearance and hygiene, along with hair style, make-up, nails, jewellery, colour co-ordination and overall manners and etiquette should be very carefully evaluated to ensure you establish a suitable image. Do not underestimate the importance of these.

How you choose to act, often in the form of voice, gestures and body language, will largely depend on what is at stake. A final interview for a coveted position or an important promotion will invariably focus your mind on communicating a desired image, a favourable attitude and a pleasing disposition. In essence you will be using a variety of techniques and tactics to present yourself in the best possible light to others. You will seek to influence and persuade others of your suitability. You will try to use your self-presentation abilities to affect the outcome, sending out signals to your audience that you possess the qualities needed for success in a particular role. You will want to show off your best features to enhance your prospects. In essence you will want others to perceive you as right for the job.

All this can be represented in terms of impression management, an increasingly important part of our social life, of our identity at work and something which has a critical impact on our future career development. If you are keen to build up a positive image, to increase your personal attractiveness, while at the same time developing your political relationships, then *impression management* will be your principal means to achieve these objectives.

PERFORMING WELL AND INFLUENCING OTHERS

Most of us will want to be seen as socially desirable. This is most important when we are engaged in influencing others to provide us with jobs and satisfying careers, We all present different faces to the world but the face we offer to a good contact or a prospective employer can be critical in promoting our future prospects. The main purpose of your impression management is to try to influence others to see you as you wish to be seen. While this may appear simple, it does raise two interesting questions which you will need to address:

■ What measures can you use to ensure that others really know about you; your professional reputation and achievements?
■ How effective will you be in putting these across to determine a successful outcome?

A useful way to approach your impression management is to

visualise it in the form of a *drama*. Indeed, many references to the way impression management is represented at work focus on its similarity to a *play*. Its key components include the actors, the audience, the stage or situation, the script, the performance and the reviews. By looking at these in more detail and from your own particular viewpoint, you will hopefully begin to understand and influence the ways you come across to others.

You as the actor

As you act out your life, you will invariably find yourself taking very different parts or roles, depending on a variety of circumstances. In one day you may find yourself being:

■ a parent
■ a job hunter
■ a counsellor or mentor
■ a friend or supportive colleague
■ a professional expert
■ a spouse or partner
■ a valued member of a club, institute or association

All these help to establish your sense of identity. This can be seen as *personal* (how you see yourself and want to be recognised) and also *social* (your place in certain social groups such as family, club, office, professional institute).

As an actor, your identity becomes important to you especially when it comes to job hunting, where you may wish to be seen as articulate, competent, innovative and energetic. Anything affecting your identity, such as redundancy, being passed over, coming second in a final interview, can be threatening and disturbing. Indeed, one of the most distressing aspects of losing your job is the loss of both your personal and social identity. You become excluded from your familiar work group, activities and surroundings and you are often forced to revise your own impressions of yourself and others as well.

Think carefully therefore about your role as *actor*, and how you present yourself and manage your performance. Thoroughly assess:

1. How your audience will react to your dress, manners, body language and verbal ability.
2. What character your audience is hoping or expecting to see. In many cases you will have already built up an image or impression of yourself from your CV or covering letter or other form of contact. Your task at interview is to build upon this impression.

Your audience

From the outset of your job search, you will begin to meet different audiences; the network contact, the search and selection consultant, the specialist agency, the careers advisor, the company recruiter, the panel interview. Each one will have different needs and expectations. Your role as actor is to address these as effectively as possible so that you can clearly establish your identity before your audience. A useful tip here is to carefully analyse what seem to you as the most important characteristics of your audience. You may find these helpful:

1. *Its status, influence and power.* Are its members of sufficient status to make decisions about employing you: can they influence your progress upwards to key decision makers?
2. *Its culture and pattern of communication.* Is it a closely knit group, linked by professional and social ties with high expectations of potential members in terms of skills and credentials; is its culture one where achievements, high performance and favourable appearance are rated highly?
3. *Its expectations of you as a job hunter.* Will your audience expect you to engage in impression management by dressing the part, displaying your knowledge, listening carefully, conforming to their values and expectations, offering appropriate compliments? Will you be telling them what they want to hear, as well as using expressive

behaviour such as a firm handshake, smiling, a warm greeting and overall politeness?

As you meet different audiences, try to break down their different features. Keep a file noting their particular needs and how you feel you can meet these. Not only will this help you to present yourself in a more structured way but it will also enable you to be one step ahead of the competition. Audience analysis, as any actor, comedian, presenter or celebrity will confirm, is an integral part of your impression management.

Your stage setting

Because you will find yourself in different settings and situations during your job search, each one has to be looked at to determine what kind of behaviour is expected of you and for what reasons. A meeting with a headhunter or a search consultant will be rather different from a panel interview or a presentation to a board of directors. Each meeting, interview, performance review, telephone conversation, or even a chance encounter in the street or on a train will build up your experience of different settings and appropriate behaviours. More importantly, they will provide you with opportunities to convey information and impressions and for others to form a judgement of your performance. In some situations your time scale is most important. You will have about four minutes at the start of an employment interview before most decisions are made about your suitability. Many presentations last between five and eight minutes, while in a leaderless group exercise you may have a mere three minutes to put over your message. When telemarketing, you may have as little as two minutes to convey the impression you are worth meeting. What all this implies is that your stage setting has to be carefully evaluated so that you can act appropriately. Each setting has its own ambience, its own distinctive layout and design, its own behaviour patterns and implicit expectations.

Your script

Your script and how you prepare and put it across is a vital part of your job search. It gives you the opportunity to convey your message, to paint a portrait of yourself and to outline your story and the personality which lies behind it. It gives you the chance not only to relate to your audience but also for your audience to respond to you, the actor. Your script also offers you the prospect of developing a particular rhythm, displaying pace and style. All this enables you to develop your particular character and to show how it relates to the overall play or drama.

Because you will be writing your own script, you will need to consider some of its important aspects; for example:

- its structure and how should this be presented in terms of sequence and timing;
- its content and how this enables the character to be developed;
- the different kinds of behaviours needed to ensure the character is convincing in the part.

Try to visualise how you will present your script within different settings. For example, what will be the form of the meeting or interview; how will it unfold; what are the expectations of the people you are going to see; what kind of behaviours are going to be most appropriate; how will you rehearse to make sure you know what message to put across?

Not only will you have to consider your interaction with your audience, but also how far you may need to improvise if you have to depart from the script. Some settings give you only a brief opportunity to present a well rehearsed script before control of the play is taken away from you, or you are stopped in your stride. Interviews do not always go as planned. You may find you do not have much scope to put across your desired image. Indeed, while sound preparation/ rehearsal is essential, prepare a back-up or contingency plan in case events do not go according to your wishes. Some of the bulletin boards on the Internet can give you interesting examples of horror stories at the interview.

Your performance

How you interact with your audience can be divided into three main parts:

■ *Your verbal behaviour* – this relates to your style of greeting, your tone of voice, accent, command of language. It also relates to your speed of speech, how quickly you react to questions, the extent of your pauses, whether you have an impediment, how far you repeat yourself and how long you talk. Also involved is your fluency and command of language, how you emphasise words and your sentence construction, how many slips of the tongue you display and how far you correct what you have said. A useful guide when responding to interview questions is to cover the main points in four to five sentences before sizing up if you think more information is required. The importance of your verbal behaviour is often highlighted when you are asked to describe yourself or a particular event; or when you are asked to give an account of your achievements or provide a detailed opinion on a special issue. Presentations, which are being increasingly used to assess verbal ability, are good opportunities for you to demonstrate your abilities as an effective communicator. They also allow you to present reasoned and coherent arguments to your audience.

■ *Your non-verbal behaviour* – this is often referred to as your body language. Besides your overall physique, it covers such aspects as your gestures, posture, eye gaze, body movement and facial expressions. Gestures come in various forms such as touching and stroking our faces, wiping our foreheads, nodding our heads, clenching our fists. They can be seen as signs of irritation or anxiety or frustration. Posture, in the ways we walk, stand and sit, position our heads, can be interpreted as being hostile and dominant, or modest and retiring, or friendly and supportive. Eye gaze is especially important. We engage in eye contact when we wish to make a point, or to observe someone or something, or to give a particular signal. We tend to look less at people we dislike and more at people we like. Within employment interviews, steady gaze is rewarded more than a shifty glance. Our facial expressions often display our emotions more accurately than our gestures and posture. We use our eyes, eyebrows and mouth to convey such emotions as anger, surprise, happiness, fear and concern. Faces not only indicate our age, race and gender, but from them we frequently make inferences about a person's intelligence or personality. If you stop to take all these into account, they combine to form an important part of your own methods of interpersonal communication. While much of your non-verbal behaviour may go unnoticed, what does alert your audience is when this becomes distorted or overemphasised or is seen as inappropriate for the occasion. Consider what you would think of someone who folded their arms during an interview, fixed you with persistent stares, slumped in their seat, gazed out of the window and drummed their fingers! *Pass or fail?*

■ *Your appearance* – this covers such issues as your clothes, dress sense, colour co-ordination, your hairstyle, make-up, whether bearded or with moustache, tattoos, rings, jewellery, and other forms of adornment. In the eyes of many selectors, these give vital clues to the way we manage our self-presentation. They convey ideas about our attitudes and abilities and whether we conform to certain stereotypes or not. In some roles, appearance is a vital part of ensuring you gain approval from others since it can highlight important cues about your personality and future work performance. The substantial expenditure on, and attention paid, to such issues as dieting, cosmetics, clothes and even plastic surgery are all good examples of our efforts to make ourselves more attractive to others. Because we see our appearance as a vital part of our image and self-esteem, we may go out of our way to seek feedback on how we look through such methods as praise, adulation or compliments. By looking the part we thus increase our prospects of achieving our desired outcome. Indeed, there is clear evidence emerging that older candidates, competing against younger ones for professional and managerial positions, are now paying far more attention to their appearance to ensure they appear attractive and remain competitive.

Your reviews

These relate to the important outcomes of your performance. Reviews show the reaction of others to your attempts at impression management. Were you successful in being selected at interview? Did you gain that vital referral to a networking contact? Did your presentation show you to be the best person for the job? Did your appraisal interview result in promotion?

Reviews are about judgements and opinions; they represent a critical survey of what you have done and how effective it has been in obtaining a particular objective. Reviews help you to learn from past mistakes and hopefully improve in the future. You may feel that some of them have been biased or prejudiced, or the reviewer has neglected to appreciate what you have to offer. For the vast majority of job hunters, rejection can be very hard to accept, especially if we feel we have made a conscious and determined effort to do our best in the circumstances. Nevertheless, handling rejection, in the same ways in which actors respond to very critical reviews, is an integral part of the job hunting process. Few of us succeed at our first attempt and several rejections may ensue before we are successful.

To help you to learn from your disappointments and rejections, here are some self-evaluation questions which you may find of value when reviewing your performance.

■ Did you take the trouble to identify the precise expectations of your audience and then go out of your way to meet and even exceed them?

- Have you carefully assessed the ways in which you relate to others, and the methods you use to provide critical insights into your abilities, personality and future potential?
- Are you aware of how others judge you and what aspects of your overall impression management create both favourable and unfavourable reactions in others?
- Do you have a chosen image of yourself and is the way you present yourself in line with your image?

You can obtain very informative feedback from carefully chosen colleagues, from spouses, partners and close friends. Seek their opinions and criticisms, and build up a dossier of those factors about yourself which both impress and fail to impress others. You can also use opportunities such as performance appraisal sessions, or actual employment interviews to obtain valuable feedback on how you come over to others and what aspects of your impression management you need to improve upon. It is only by doing this that you can obtain what is termed 'a rich picture' of *your total corporate image*.

THE TACTICS OF IMPRESSION MANAGEMENT

In the past you may have made mistakes in failing to sell yourself in a critical interview. You may have missed a good opportunity to enhance your profile during a presentation or within a performance review. You may also have alienated the wrong people, failed to build important alliances with colleagues or ignored the negative impact you had on powerful superiors or outside contacts. All these contribute to your overall reputation and this in turn affects your promotion prospects, your career development and your job satisfaction. You will have seen colleagues whose behaviour often antagonises, confuses or even frustrates others. They become typecast or stereotyped by their previous encounters. It has been very clearly established that people seen as the antithesis of the specific culture of an organisation will soon be rejected. This applies particularly so when changes at the top of an organisation herald the creation of a new culture. Those whose behaviours do not reflect what is needed in the new ways of doing things should not expect to remain for long. The frequently used expression 'new boss, new job' is very apt in these circumstances.

Just as encounters between buyers and sellers are critical, so your encounters within the changing world of work are crucial for your own success. Whatever the nature of the encounter we immediately form impressions of others, even on very sketchy or minimal information. Most of these impressions can be described as personality traits, in that we judge people as friendly or hostile, cold introvert or extrovert. Some people will try hard to control how others see them. They will not reveal their real identity or they will present different aspects of their personality according to their audience. Others will go out of their way to present themselves in a particular image, especially during interaction with a superior at work. They will be good at openly and spontaneously expressing their emotions through facial expressions. They will use a range of verbal tactics to impress through speech, tone, accent, emphasis and clarity of expression. Their gaze, body posture and gestures all seem well co-ordinated to give a heightened view of their competence, presence, and self-confidence.

You may well ask therefore, *how do they do it?* Are there tactics or approaches which you can use to improve your own impression management, and are these really worth the effort? To try and answer these questions, let us examine three popular *tactics* in a little more detail.

Tactic 1 – the art of ingratiation

This involves a range of behaviours designed to bring you into favour with others. It is not about being devious or manipulative or becoming a 'yes person'. Rather is it about making an effort to be more attractive and better liked. If your motivation is to be seen in a highly favourable light during your job hunting and afterwards, then the art of ingratiation is likely to bring positive benefits. For example, if you are currently employed but are after promotion, you will advance your prospects by being seen as someone who is agreeable, likeable, considerate and desirable as a friend. If you are currently seeking another role, then you should be demonstrating these self-enhancing attributes during the selection process. Being recognised as someone who sincerely praises others, who pays appropriate compliments, who does favours in a subtle way — these are all part of ingratiation. They are tactics you can use to considerable effect if you wish to be seen as someone who fosters goodwill and develops harmonious working relationships, especially when work is highly team or project centred Taking a genuine interest in the performance and personal life of superiors, as well as supporting their actions and conforming to their opinions (when this is opportune) can also bring recognition. This is often seen as an invaluable part of building alliances and power networks, while at the same time showing how far you agree with prevailing policies and opinions. Being sensitive and attuned to the social and political environment within any organisation is again part of the ingratiation process. Do not simply regard this as merely sycophantic or even blatantly altruistic. Some audiences will both encourage and welcome ingratiation more than others. Clearly understanding what signals are effective in influencing others is a vital skill for aspiring managers and professionals. Dressing the part, saying the right things and using skilful flattery are just some of the well-established conventions in the modern workplace. Indeed, these may be the most important parts of your impression management repertoire. We all have a desire to be liked; using and accepting ingratiation tactics is part of the process of making yourself more appealing.

Tactic 2 – the art of self-promotion

If ingratiation is showing yourself to be pleasing and likeable, *self-promotion* is about your competence and effective performance in a particular job. Here the emphasis is very different. It is based partly on the premise that no one gives you a job simply because they like you. Instead, selectors will be keen to know as much as possible about your skills and intelligence, vital factors which bring benefits to an employer and contribute to your success in a role or within a team or on a project. Because your hard-won credentials and your work performance will be very much on public view, you will be using self-promotion to make the best of yourself. You will need to be convincing to your audience, demonstrating assurance, showing you are a winner and portraying your expertise and professionalism. Where you are laying claims to a particular job, you will need to convince others that you are a legitimate and worthwhile prospect. A tried and tested strategy is to focus on two highly interdependent issues: *what are you going to say* and *how are you going to say it*.

What are you going to say?

This concerns selecting those aspects of your past performance and future potential which will create the most desirable impression of yourself. Here are ten performance issues, in the form of FAQs, which you should address by compiling concise answers, with appropriate examples, against each one.

1. How do you conduct yourself at work? Describe your interpersonal relations in a group or team.
2. What is your preferred management style and how effective is it in building a successful team?
3. In what ways are your skills relevant and up-to-date, or have they reached their sell-by date?
4. How far do your credentials and recent achievements clearly match the jobs you are seeking?

5. What have been your recent personal successes and how will you repeat these in the future?
6. What goals are you set at work: how far do you achieve them and within what time scale?
7. Which of your verbal and non-verbal reasoning abilities are most likely to affect your performance?
8. What is your approach to problem solving at work and how do you cope when things go wrong?
9. Which aspects of your track record to date may be a cause for concern or show you in a poor light?
10. What do your performance reports indicate about you and your future prospects?

You will notice that these are related to the ways in which you establish your reputation and credibility. They relate to the work you did and the jobs held in previous organisations, as well as reports and appraisals of your performance. These are in no way exhaustive and you should compile a list of your own competencies and performance attributes which you feel can give you a competitive advantage. Rehearse these to make sure you are both fluent and convincing. Look at adverts and job specifications to gain a greater insight into the competencies seen as both essential and desirable in particular jobs. Selectors frequently ask probing and penetrating questions in an attempt to gain a clear picture of your previous performance and abilities, This is because they will need to be convinced these are relevant before making a job offer. If you fail to convince, or there are lingering doubts about your performance, then you will be rejected. By analysing the key performance indicators within each job you are considering, you can then set about determining what you are going to say and will be well on the way to improving the impressions you make on others.

How are you going to say it?

This involves the different ways in which you verbally communicate what you have to offer. It is your opportunity to make yourself look good through your verbal skills. Let us look at a typical opening question used extensively by selectors, namely:

'Why don't we begin by you telling me a little about yourself'.

Here is your chance to set the scene, to disclose important aspects of yourself and to establish a rapport between yourself and your audience. You will need to structure your reply, assessing what the question means, why is it so frequently asked and what aspects of yourself are likely to show you as a superior performer. You could consider such issues as:

■ your personality – how far you are creative, conscientious, persistent, imaginative, single minded;
■ your related experience – how far it mirrors what is needed, how broad or how specific and detailed;
■ your capacity to learn quickly and grow into a job without too much supervision and training;
■ your individual management style and determination to motivate and lead others;
■ your ability to meet and exceed targets while impressing customers and colleagues.

This question is frequently answered badly, with candidates giving personal rather than performance details. Relate your concise answer to what you consider the interviewer expects to hear. Then demonstrate where you have made a personal and important contribution to profit margins, cost reductions, change programmes, introducing new technologies, problem solving, turnarounds, quality initiatives. If you are just setting out on the first stage of your career, relate your achievements during training or at college or university, endeavouring to show how the lessons learned can be effectively transferred.

Your verbal performance is vital in communicating your desired image. Here are several important ways in which you can do this during the selection process.

1. *Self-description* – here you disclose aspects of yourself which may be very important for future job performance such as special abilities, feelings, opinions, behaviour patterns and personality traits.

2. *Providing accounts of yourself* – how you performed certain tasks, made certain decisions, left one job to go to another, came to be where you are now, took part in a special event or project.
3. *Enhancing your claim* – showing your level and degree of responsibility, taking personal credit, indicating specific and verifiable achievements, giving examples of obstacles overcome, contracts won.
4. *Complimenting others* – indicating support from your colleagues and appearing team-centred with phrases like 'without team backing and commitment I would not have accomplished....'
5. *Bestowing favours on colleagues* – recognising performance in others and rewarding this through appropriate symbolic gestures such as 'once the merger was finalised, I took my team to lunch....'

Selectors will often infer a range of personal characteristics after hearing your verbal performance. Being seen as articulate and logical, competent and self-confident, ambitious and intelligent, all arise out of your verbal aptitude. This can be broken down into several factors such as your accent and speech errors, your speech rate and fluency, your volume and clarity, your tone and emphasis and your speed of response and reaction time. Other factors include how you co-ordinate your speech with your body movement, how long you take to describe events, how you use words and phrases. All these provide important clues to your social status, educational level, and cultural group as well as your self-confidence, friendliness and competencies. Since your speech is frequently seen as important in displaying your trustworthiness, sense of humour and personal integrity, your verbal performance should receive very careful attention.

Tactic 3 – the art of non-verbal behaviour

Your non-verbal behaviour (NVB), while clearly different from your speech, is also an integral part of your ability to impress others. NVB essentially refers to how you act in terms of your facial expressions, your gestures and postures, your eye contact, and the ways in which you move and position your body. It is often referred to as expressive behaviour because people will usually infer from your NVB that you are expressing aspects of your personality. Meeting others for the first time, you may be quickly summed up as warm and friendly, or cold and aloof. What you will be doing is giving important cues to others who are perceiving you. For example, you may be good at expressing your emotions (such as joy, anxiety, boredom, enthusiasm) through facial expressions. Alternatively, you may feel inhibited in disclosing your feelings and will not act openly and spontaneously. You may not smile readily, or engage in handshaking or you will try to avoid frequent eye contact.

What is significant in your NVB is that what you intend to convey through gestures or looks may be taken to mean something rather different by those whom you meet.The difficulty which we all face is that we tend to be better at judging others as opposed to judging how others see us. What emerges very clearly is that much of your NVB and how you choose to display it can be judged quite superficially by others. Irrespective whether this is right or wrong, an impression can be very quickly established about yourself in terms of:

- *your mood or emotional state* − for example are you happy, irritated, flustered, calm, impatient or tired;
- *your reactions* − are you seen as fair or brusque, curt or welcoming, friendly or unsupportive;
- *your attitude* − are you regarded as bored, pompous, sceptical, cynical, receptive.

However such opinions are formed, from even brief samples of your NVB, they will invariably affect the way others will behave towards you. You may be regarded as reliable and trustworthy and given a position of responsibility in handling large amounts of investment. Alternatively, you may be giving unfavourable signals that label you as immature or indecisive.

Because you will be very much in the public eye when you

are involved in job hunting, your public behaviour will be most important in ensuring you achieve your goals or objectives. How you come across to others (ie your audience or target) will be critical simply because you will be heavily reliant on them to bestow favours, or open doors, or confirm appointments. Once in the public arena, the stakes become higher and so does your motivation. Not only is your identity, self-esteem and reputation often on the line, but so are the material outcomes such as jobs, promotions, performance appraisal and even building sound network contacts for the future. Failure or rejection may cause you to cast doubt on your abilities and skills. Therefore it becomes imperative that you increase your efforts to improve your NVB by carefully analysing those aspects which are most likely to create a favourable impression with your audience.

USING BODY LANGUAGE TO ENHANCE YOUR PROSPECTS

To help you to sell yourself, carefully consider how you will use your face, your posture and your gestures as part of your plan to develop *your total corporate image*.

1. *Your facial behaviour* provides signals which far outweigh your gestures and postures. Your face conveys much information that will be of value to those who are assessing you. It displays your age, gender, race, even your social class and level of attractiveness. It is also your special means by which you identify yourself and endeavour to influence others. Because you are known by your face, you can exert a greater control over your facial expressions than any other forms of your NVB. By using your eyebrows, lips, mouth, eyes, nose and teeth, you will be able to convey your mood, your intentions, your motivation and how attentive and interested you are. Your visual cues are far more likely to outweigh your

verbal ones in establishing your acceptability for the job. High levels of eye gaze in an interview builds up your credibility and assurance, while looking away can indicate disinterest and uninvolvement. A steady gaze is often seen as a sign of honesty, sincerity and persuasiveness, provided of course that you have been introduced. Otherwise it can be interpreted as threatening and hostile. If you are seeking approval from a selector, then you should endeavour to engage in a higher smile rate, since this will often convey you as open, trustworthy and confident. By employing friendly facial expressions, establishing eye contact about 60 per cent of the discussion time, and looking more frequently when actually addressing someone, you will find that these lead to increased ratings on such issues as trust, respect, dependability and being seen as extrovert rather than introvert.

2. *Your posture*, especially the ways in which you sit and stand, is capable of conveying very different messages to your audience. Consider how you would interpret someone whom you were interviewing for a position, and who sat down with arms crossed, legs splayed apart, toes tapping persistently, trunk occasionally swivelling and shoulders frequently shrugging in response to questions. While this may seem an extreme case, it is through your body posture that you are able to show if you are attentive and motivated. Your body language will also show if you are indifferent and suspicious, or assertive and dominant. Considerable attention has been given to body movement by means of a technique called action profiling; this attempts to show links between your movement behaviour and how far you will be successful as a professional, in terms of communicating your intentions, presenting your ideas, being adaptable and displaying commitment and dynamism. Here are a few examples to show how your own posture is capable of being interpreted.

Your posture	How it may be interpreted
Folding your arms	Seen as defensive, self-protective and withdrawn
Shrugging your shoulders	Seen as indifferent, indecisive, helpless
Drooping, listless and languid trunk	Seen as inadequate, lacking in drive and energy
Sitting primly, on the edge of your seat	Seen as anxious, nervous, humble, accommodating
Leaning back in seat, hands supporting head	Seen as showing authority, superiority, haughtiness
Sitting upright, then leaning slightly forward	Seen as interested, motivated, involved, positive
Crossing legs at knee, toes pointing down	Seen as standard interview posture; shows confidence
Locked ankles alongside clenched hands	Seen as showing anxiety, apprehension, tension

3. *Your gestures* are specific body movements such as nodding your head, touching and stroking your face, wiping your forehead, putting your hand over your mouth, expansive use of your hands and forearms, patting on the back, shaking hands and waving. Within an interview they can be quite revealing, showing anxiety, impatience or approval. Nevertheless you can use them to good effect. By tilting your head on one side you can show interest. By carefully nodding you can show enthusiasm, give encouragement and indicate agreement. Your gestures not only indicate your excitement or level of interest, you can also use them to good effect to reinforce your arguments or emphasise your line of thought. Indeed, those with greater verbal fluency also tend to use more gestures in order to add to their persuasiveness. Special attention has been given to the importance of the

handshake as a conventional gesture. Ensure yours is firm but not crushing or overemphasised. Check your palm is not perspiring and co-ordinate this with direct eye contact and a straight, sincere gaze. This will help to emphasise that you are serious and also have an air of authority.

In conclusion, you need to consider what aspects of yourself you are trying to project in order to develop *your total corporate image*. These will vary, but you may find that you tend to concentrate on your personality and personal attributes rather than your physical appearance and attractiveness. Again you may focus on your role and achievements, or the values and beliefs that you hold, or your contacts and association with other people or groups. Whatever approach you adopt, do bear in mind that impression management is *not* about pretence, or falsehoods or flattery. Neither is it about opportunism. Rather it is about what you need to do to project the best of yourself when you appear on public view. For it is then that you are under scrutiny and subject to the judgement of others. Conveying the right impression increases your prospects of a desired outcome.

TEN TIPS TO IMPROVE YOUR IMPRESSION MANAGEMENT

- *Tip 1* – after each employment or networking interview, obtain as much feedback as possible about your performance. Ask about the key issues which determined how decisions were made; where you may have gone wrong; how you can improve next time; what impressions you gave and how you can manage these more effectively in the future. Open a file detailing these, then take action to remedy any faults. This is all part of your *damage repair*.
- *Tip 2* – seek the opinions of close colleagues, relatives and friends whose views you value and trust in terms of how you they see you and how you could improve the image you wish to project. Listen carefully to their comments and

criticisms, but endeavour to see these as constructive and helpful rather than hurtful and damaging to your ego and self-confidence.

■ *Tip 3* – critically review all aspects of your impression management strategy. Adopt a profit and loss account approach, establishing which ones add value to your application and which ones could lead to rejection. Then devise a strategy to improve your shortcomings. You could work harder on your appearance; take elocution lessons; practise short, punchy replies to standard interview questions; avoid irritating or off-putting habits.

■ *Tip 4* – construct a check list of the qualities by which you would wish to be seen, such as decisive, determined, energetic. Then ask how others see you – dogmatic, cynical, superior! If there is considerable variation, ask others how they would wish you to alter your behaviour.

■ *Tip 5* – draw up a comprehensive list of your key achievements. Against each one, establish what was the problem, how you approached it, how you decided on the solution and what was the outcome. Sort them into priority order, and rehearse them so that they come to mind quickly and easily when you are asked to give an account of yourself.

■ *Tip 6* – establish a list of key phrases, words and abbreviations that form the 'tech-speak' within your particular field or profession. Understand precisely what they mean, keep up to date with new examples (very important in the IT world) and use them sparingly but appropriately when meeting selectors or establishing contacts.

■ *Tip 7* – what you say is only the tip of the iceberg. When you meet someone for the first time, it is your immediate behaviour (frequent smiling, firm and dry handshake, not wimpish and wet, high level of gaze, maintaining eye contact) which will convey to others your competence and strength of character.

■ *Tip 8* – practise showing your liking for other people, no matter how hard this may seem. Express interest in their activities, seek out common experiences, offer gestures of goodwill. You will be quite surprised by the positive reaction that you will receive.

■ *Tip 9* – have a friend conduct, and record on video, a series of mock interviews about 20 minutes each. Adopt a critical stance of your appearance, facial expressions, mannerisms, speech patterns and posture. In particular, check how well you performed in the first four minutes. Then go over the process at least three times to see how far you are correcting any glaring mistakes.

■ *Tip 10* – collect from colleagues and friends a set of searching and difficult questions. Then construct answers to each one, ensuring these are concise and accurate. Use this to display your competence and to demonstrate your technical and communication skills. This is your chance to show others what you know (*expertise*) and what you can deliver (*performance*).

5

Networking: The Inside Track to Contacts, Information and Influence

INTRODUCTION

The bottom line is that cultivating the right contacts can help you get what you want out of life.'

Cynthia Chin-Lee

Networking lies at the heart of your employability. Used effectively, it can produce a rich mixture of excitement, challenge, interest and reward. In addition, through networking you can often unearth a range of enterprising and sometimes remarkable leads that enable you to discover hidden job opportunities with surprising results. It is also a vital ingredient not only in sustaining your own morale and motivation, but also in the long term development of your reputation and your career. However, as with all forms of job search, if you are to turn it into a successful strategy, you will need a high degree of planning and organisation as well as sensitivity and persistence. In this chapter we aim to show how you can do this.

Think of networks as chains of interconnected persons, with each individual in the network having certain links or pathways to other members of the network. The pathways become conduits along which flows information, resources and influence. Contact between members, which may be frequent or intermittent, will differ in intensity, in pattern and in relevance. The specific characteristics of a network largely depend on the type of relationship that connects different people together. You may have family networks, while others may be professional or based on social ties. Members of professional networks often find them attractive because they help in sharing ideas, experiences and problems as well as in counteracting isolation and distance. You can do this to some extent by using bulletin boards on the Internet. Within work organisations, relations may be based on such issues as leadership, friendship, professional or occupational ties, advice-giving or information holding. As you begin to investigate networks in your job hunting, you will find they vary in size and geographic location, in behaviour and attitude, and also in the strength of ties between members.

You will also discover that networks vary in the help and support they can offer you in both your job search and career development. This is because they differ quite markedly in prestige and status, in power and influence and in their openness and accessibility. Some are easy to enter, and reaching a key decision maker will be a relatively smooth experience. Others are close-knit and hidebound; they are manned by gatekeepers who make it difficult to penetrate without an influential contact.

WHY NETWORKS ARE IMPORTANT

Networks are especially important because they affect *access* to three critical factors in your job hunting and overall career development.

- *Information* – indicating developments in sectors and organisations before they become well known.
- *Resources* – providing an entre to decision-makers looking to recruit managers and professionals.
- *Influence* – building relationships, forming attitudes, shaping opinions and enhancing reputations.

Over the last 25 years, research findings by academics and outplacement consultants consistently support the idea that networks are critically important in your effective job hunting. For example, between 60 per cent and 80 per cent of managerial and professional groups attribute their success in job hunting to their network prowess. Even for post-graduates the figure can be as high as 50 per cent; this rises sharply as people move into their second and third jobs. So, why should you consider networking and is it an appropriate strategy for your own personal needs?

■ Members of networks not only collect and disseminate information about jobs; they also make decisions about who should fill them; by accessing them you can often overcome tight candidate profiles, costly and time consuming selection procedures, and even create your own job.

■ The recruitment of new members, especially into growing small to medium sized organisations, is predominantly by means of the network ties of their existing members rather than by other methods such as advertising, agencies or direct application.

■ In organisations where the 'changing of the guard' is a continuous reality, recruitment from outside through network ties can be a speedy and low cost solution to skills shortages and the need to quickly bring in new ideas and approaches to productivity and problem-solving.

You will realise from these that networking is essentially *instrumental*. You set out to make contacts so that you obtain information, ideas and advice about possible vacancies and about recruitment and selection criteria. However, for a large proportion of jobs, information about their whereabouts within the labour market is not readily and freely available to all. Advertisements may attempt to reach as wide an audience as possible of appropriately qualified and available applicants. Yet these account only for a relatively small number of vacancies and for many employers they are expensive and often used only as a last resort.

So, you may ask, where are all these jobs? The answer is that many are confined to what is called *the hidden job market*, a term used to describe the situation where information about vacancies is not for public consumption and where network-based recruitment is the norm. These jobs are not so much hidden or indeed inaccessible, rather are they simply out of sight to those who may superficially see the job market composed only of advertised vacancies. In this case, what you see is not necessarily what you get. The reality of networking is that the actual number of people considered for positions may be severely restricted and their screening and selection is invariably in the hands of a small number of individuals. The network thus becomes the decision-making environment about job allocation. It provides insider information in matching individuals to job vacancies. *It is both the 'job tipper' and the 'job controller'.*

BUILDING YOUR OWN NETWORK

From the outset, if you wish to be serious about networking and fully exploit its considerable potential, you need to design and build your own personal network. This is essentially a web of *'friends of friends, contacts of contacts'*. Your task is to continually assess and evaluate it in order to see how far it can be of value to you in your job hunting and, more importantly, in your future career development. Almost all successful job hunters have a well developed network which is continually refined, analysed and utilised to help them achieve their career goals. Once you have built your network, then you also need to maintain and service it to ensure it will meet your future needs. Look upon your network as both a resource centre and a safety net in case you are unexpectedly out of work.

First-time job hunters will usually have far less developed networks than those who have changed jobs several times over a period of time. Before embarking on the outline design of your network, you need to clarify the difference between a primary contact and a referral. A primary contact is literally anyone you know whom you feel may be of assistance in your job search. Contacts become vital links in accessing networks through intermediaries or referrals. Thus a referral is anyone to whom you are referred by a primary contact. This may come about by personal recommendation or formal introduction. A simple illustration showing both short and long network chains is given below:

primary contact → referral → access to network decision-maker → job offer made and accepted

primary contact → referral access to network → member unable to make final decision → passed on to next referral in network chain → eventually reaching decision maker → job offer made and accepted

Your outline design can be quite simple to start with and then refined over a period of time to give you a very detailed picture of the extent and potential of your network. You can use software which specialises in the production of organisational charts, or you can incorporate details of your contacts on spreadsheets or databases. Much will depend on your competence in these areas as well as the size of your contact list. To begin with, construct a simple chart with four basic categories as suggested below. Then brainstorm with others who may be able to help and build up a series of sub-categories with names, addresses and telephone numbers. Your network may then begin to look something like this:

■ *Friends, relatives and acquaintances* — family members and their friends — neighbours and their friends — school, university, college contacts — Christmas card lists
■ *Social and cultural* — sports and social clubs — church or religious groups — local community groups — recreational or hobby groups — educational classes — PTA, support groups — drama or theatrical or musical associations — ramblers and drivers — drinkers and holiday makers — contacts at weddings, parties, even funerals,
■ *Professional and business* — associates past and present — associations such as Round Table, Ladies Circle, Rotary Clubs, Chamber of Commerce — professional associations

(lawyers, bankers, accountants, medicine, dentistry, engineers) – Women in Business – luncheon clubs – business suppliers – competitors – other job searchers – industry dinners – in-house events and celebrations

■ *Other forms of association* – conventions – conferences – exhibitions – meetings – business cards collected – members of courses attended as well as organisers and tutors – former career advisors – consultants – discussion groups – workshops – visits to organisations and events

Tackle this interesting task with vigour even if it takes you some time to compose. While it will reflect your own interests and social contacts, try to be imaginative in its construction and bear in mind that the larger the number of primary contacts the greater the chances of referral into a productive network.

When the initial list has been mapped out, you can then begin the more serious task of evaluating just who is worthy of an early approach. For this you need to develop a set of criteria such as:

■ Who understands your current needs and is able to offer constructive advice and referral names?

■ Who, because of their current occupation and position, is likely to provide access to a developed network related to your own particular interests?

■ Who is likely to be supportive, approachable, encouraging and informative?

■ Who has the prestige, status and influence to be able to link up with a decision-maker in a network?

■ What is the strength of tie between your contact and the referral – is it strong or weak and does it have the potential to lead to a decision maker?

These are not easy issues to resolve and you need to be diplomatic and highly selective in your choice of contacts, especially if you are changing industry or even occupation. Some will not produce the referrals you are seeking and will fail to help you at a critical time. Don't be disappointed or give up.

It is all part of the learning process within networking. In any case, you are likely to receive plenty of rejections when answering advertisements, and your chances within networking are usually considerably better.

The key issue in networking is straightforward; your initial focus should be far less on the person you know and far more on those who know the person. In other words, who does your contact know whose reputation is established, whose opinion is respected and whose recommendation is taken seriously?

An interesting piece of recent research has indicated that it can take twenty five times longer to find a job when you start your search without any kind of network. If you are just about to start looking for your first managerial job or professional appointment, or entering the labour market after a lengthy period of training, then you may find that your contact list is rather small. Nevertheless, even with a relatively sparse network you soon begin to enhance your prospects quite considerably. Indeed, almost all of us start off with a small network and build upon it as we move from job to job. The important point here is to utilise the resources of the networks with which you come in contact with imagination, tact and confidence.

Two tips which you may find of particular value in building your own network, are:

1. Find two or three established persons in different fields of interest and ask them about their own network – how they started – how they keep it up-to-date and productive – what advice can they pass on – what lessons have they learned on the way. Then check this against your own network outline and ideas and see if you can improve upon it. You may even produce a number of versions of your networking design to use at different stages of your job search. Test them on friends and colleagues.

2. Design a network contact card or worksheet which provides a range of information which you will need, not just for your next position, but throughout your career. Work on A3 paper to start with, and experiment with

spider diagrams or decision trees or flow diagrams. Keep revising it by adding and deleting people with whom you come in contact. Collecting business cards is quite common, but you can also record meetings, conversations, conference members, reports in the press, articles in journals, job advertisements (often have a contact name), trade magazines. Include sections for ideas, developments, contact suggestions; use an organiser or similar software to store your results.

Always have this information readily accessible. Endeavour to make it an essential part of your search strategy, in the same way as keeping your CV up-to-date. By doing this you ensure that you are fully prepared for networking in case your current position unexpectedly comes to an end or you find that your current prospects are not quite what they seemed. *The need for effective networking by professionals and managers is likely to increase significantly in the future, especially for those who are establishing portfolio careers. This is because the life expectancy of jobs is set to decline while the populations of organisations will continue to alter in size and composition.*

TARGETING AND RESEARCHING POTENTIAL SOURCES OF JOBS

Networks can be visualised as information highways along which you travel over a period of time before gaining access to a particular job market. The ease with which information and ideas will flow along the highway will often depend on two factors. These are the frequency of contact and the level of trust and confidence which exists between members of the network. Certain networks may contain a substantial number of intermediaries whom you go through before reaching a decision maker. Decision makers are invariably facilitators, people who make things happen and who themselves are proficient networkers and understand your approach. In other networks you can reach a decision maker on your first attempt. Much will depend on the structure of the organisation and the membership and expertise of the network. Your aim in networking is to maximise your chances of finding contacts and referrals who, together, will hopefully become vital sources of job information and influence. Access to a network is rather like finding a window of opportunity in the job market. With care and good management, it will provide the entré to a job which matches your skills and aspirations.

The next stage of your plan involves bringing together several strands of activities. These are:

1. Sending an abbreviated CV (a one-page resume will probably suffice) together with a one-page covering letter to all your chosen primary contacts, to whom you have previously spoken about your plans. The focus should be on your goals, achievements and skills and what you can offer a potential employer in terms of problem solving, enhancing performance and team development. The emphasis should be on demonstrating your employability and what makes you professionally unique in terms of added value. Thank them for their support, however small, and always report your progress to them.

2. Once you establish a link with a referral, then you engage in a similar way by suggesting you send a well-designed, abbreviated CV with a one page covering letter outlining similar issues to those in 1. above. Do not push hard at this stage since it may appear that you are job hunting rather than seeking information and advice. Assuming your CV will be welcomed, put in it an indication of your expectations, experience and any quantifiable outcomes of your work. In your letter you should indicate the purpose of the meeting, how you feel your referral may be of assistance and give an idea of the kind of opening you are seeking. Your documentation should give a strong indication of your problem solving abilities. You will be offered a position not because someone likes you but because you can solve their problems.

3. Once the referral invites you for a discussion, then you begin to prepare thoroughly for the referral meeting; other terms are the information or networking interview. Think carefully about such issues as: why are we meeting; what kind of questions should I be posing and for what purpose; what do I need to discover to enable me to progress to the next stage?

THE REFERRAL MEETING

Sound preparation is of the essence. This is irrespective whether it is your first referral meeting or whether you are well along a particular chain and about to meet a key decision maker with a potential job to offer. You will need to determine a number of important factors before you attend. For example:

■ What is the exact purpose of the meeting? Is it fact finding, exploratory, investigative, the first in a long chain? Is it to let others know of your availability or do you wish to retain confidentiality?

■ How do you determine its structure and timing? If it is only 20 minutes long, how do you use it to your advantage? What is the best way of structuring your questions and how much talking should you do compared with the person you are meeting, perhaps for the first time?

■ Will you be meeting a key decision maker or are you using it as a method of finding one within the network? Will it be a useful way of improving your interview skills? Will it turn into an interview?

Underlining all these questions is the need for sound preparation, thorough research and data-retrieval in well stocked and specialist commercial libraries. The use of various on-line services (eg Compuserve, AmericaOnline, Delphi) as well as the Internet browsers Netscape or MSN, which provide access to the world wide web, can also be very effective. Chapter Six provides further details to help you.

Within the meeting, while making clear your goals and overall direction, endeavour to structure the discussion around three main criteria:

1. *Advice* – which organisations have problems that you could help to solve? What are their entry requirements in terms of credentials, skills and personal qualities? Who may have vacancies in your sector? What sectors or organisations to avoid or to target? Is your CV and general approach to job search acceptable? How could it be improved upon? What are the current and longer term prospects like in your area?

2. *Information* – who is expanding, contracting, moving, merging, retiring, restructuring, downsizing, outsourcing, leaving? What technological developments are taking place? Where are the contracts going? When are new products coming to market? What initiatives are happening in your special area? What trends and ideas are fashionable? What challenges lie ahead and how would your performance be assessed?

3. *Next referral* – To whom should you be talking next? Who are the catalysts who make things happen? What is their position or status, and what special issues and interests should you raise when seeing them? Ideally you should be coming away with at least one name. If you don't, then that particular network may have run its course and you will then look to your remaining referrals. Sometimes a referral will not divulge another source during the meeting but will leave time to establish contact with other network members before coming back to you.

UNDERSTANDING THE RULES OF THE GAME

If you are to use networking effectively, certain rules of behaviour do apply, in the sense that you are playing a game according to agreed rules. These can be summarised as follows:

- Do not ask for a job; it may just not be available at that time and it may need to be created to fit your particular skills as well as the operational requirements of the organisation.
- Always invite suggestions; continually seek feedback on your approach and progress.
- Follow up all leads and leave nothing to chance. Offers can arise from quite unusual sources.
- Always send thank you letters promptly, expressing gratitude and promising to keep the person aware of your progress. Be meticulous in this in order to build mutual confidence and respect.
- Keep control of any meeting, unless you feel it is turning into an interview, in which case control will normally be in the hands of the interviewer. Instead of you talking 25 per cent of the time, this could quickly become 75 per cent. In any referral meeting you are principally the recipient of ideas and information.
- Ensure you have some definite objective in mind such as an issue to explore; an idea to develop; a proposition to present; or a skill to display. Keeping the initiative is your own responsibility and you must not hesitate to close a meeting quite early if you sense it is becoming a time-wasting exercise.
- Continually check you are clearly indicating your goals and transferable skills to the people you meet.

From what has been discussed so far, you could be forgiven for assuming that all this activity is highly instrumental and one-sided. *'What's in it for me'* may appear to be the underlying aim but this is far from the reality of networking. The underlying principle is a simple one. *How can you help this person or organisation rather than how can this person or organisation help you.* It is only when key decision makers in the referral chain perceive that by helping you they are also helping themselves that they will be willing to see you and indeed offer an appointment. Throughout the networking process the issues of trust and confidence becomes essential. While it may seem like reciprocal back-scratching on the surface, network-based selection is practised because of its overall advantages to the organisation concerned.

DRAWBACKS AND PROBLEMS

In statistical terms, approaching your job search from only one perspective, namely networking, may seem to be very effective. After all, up to 80 per cent of managerial and professional roles may be filled through network-based recruitment. However, over-estimating its significance and what it can do for you can lead to disappointment and disillusionment. At the outset, try to bear in mind that networking, like all methods of job search in a fast-moving and uncertain labour market, can have drawbacks.

■ You, and others around you, may perceive this instrumental approach to be unacceptable. It may be seen as soliciting, begging or crawling; it may look as if you are taking advantage of others or that you can't find a job on your own; it may seem unprofessional or even underhand.

■ It may require a certain type of personality (outgoing, gregarious, controlled, friendly, imaginative and quick to establish rapport) which you may not possess and which you would find hard to represent in any referral meeting. Again, you may fear embarrassment or rejection; since this could threaten your dependency position, you may not feel comfortable going down this route.

■ You may not wish to advertise your intentions in case your employer discovers your plans, and uses this as an excuse to dispense with your services.

■ In some labour markets, especially in the public sector, there may be strict regulations relating to informal and deliberate job search by networking or contact development. The notice *canvassing in any form will disqualify* may still apply in a formal sense, though many successful candidates will already have established critical contacts well before the vacancy arises.

- The *whom you know* approach is just not good enough to generate productive leads. You enter networks where there are too many job seekers and too few vacancies. Your meetings are with people who have neither the motivation nor influence to help you and you find yourself in a dead end.

- Finally, be aware of the potential pitfalls in relying solely on families or friends for network contacts. You need to avoid embarrassing situations, or prejudicing long established friendships. What is often at stake is both your reputation and theirs. For the sake of your future career, you will doubtless wish to be selected on objective and measurable performance criteria rather than on family influence and contacts.

All these objections are real and justifiable, but they have to be seen in the overall context of your commitment to job hunting and your own personal drive and motivation. It is all too easy to be apprehensive about networking, to rely on sending out written applications for 'real' (ie advertised) jobs and to wait for contacts to come to you. The simple answer is, it is very unlikely that this will happen either now or in the next few years. *Being proactive says something about you, about your self-marketing and research skills, about your creativity and persistence, about your interpersonal skills and ability to make things happen. Within a job, all these factors are critically important when others are evaluating your performance.*

Networking is one very good way of demonstrating these qualities to those charged with recruitment and selection. The solution is to undertake your networking in an organised, systematic and enthusiastic way, following the points made earlier, and continually learning from your experiences. In the present climate, no other approach provides you with the same opportunity to determine your own progress, your own marketing strategy and to create your own job.

To summarise, successful networking requires:

- Focusing on those who have something to offer in terms of vacancies and opportunities.
- Constantly keeping in touch with contacts and referrals, relaying progress and gaining feedback.
- Researching the market to find the greatest potential outlets for your skills and aspirations.
- Analysing your needs and communicating your goals to referrals to gain trust and respect.
- Being creative, imaginative and persistent while remaining optimistic, cheerful and polite.
- Adopting a 'project management approach', involving planning, research, implementation and review so that you achieve a successful outcome.

CONTACT DEVELOPMENT THROUGH TARGETED ORGANISATIONS

Networking clearly does not constitute the entire or complete approach to job search. Research also strongly supports another quite similar method, namely *contact development through targeted organisations*. When linked to networking, this enables you to approach a wider range of potential employing organisations. In effect, although it is still speculative, it will rapidly increase the *number of irons you have in the fire*.

Your targeting will involve two main approaches. First, researching those organisations which you consider have internal labour markets that are likely to take people with your skills and experience. Secondly, identifying a key person within the organisation who is likely to be interested in what you have to offer and who will give you the opportunity to outline your proposals in a face to face discussion. Watch for people who are on the move, or making key speeches or addresses at conferences or symposiums, or writing articles or publicising themselves and their organisations.

Successful targeting depends on a variety of factors which you need to take into account when undertaking your research.

The following are given as guides so that your search will become more manageable and more productive.

■ Does your target organisation have formal rules and procedures about recruitment which may limit your chances of entry; are there strict requirements concerning age, gender, qualifications, skill levels, pensions and retirement and if so, are you able to meet most or all of these?

■ Is the organisation large, centralised, bureaucratic, with perhaps a few points of entry at a low level, and where promotion and vacancies are normally filled from within? If so, it is very likely to have its own internal labour market, and entry may be difficult unless you have a very rare set of special skills.

■ Does the organisation recruit locally or nationally, and is recruitment in the hands of central personnel or individual senior managers? Is there emphasis on grades and performance, tests and job descriptions? Is it family owned or private, or is it a plc, with an established reputation?

■ What is its size in employees and capitalisation, and does this affect its hiring decisions? Does it operate in a fast moving environment and rely heavily on information and skills in order to solve problems?

Bear in mind that all these issues affect an organisation's capacity to recruit from direct approaches or to stock up in advance with people with employable skills. When establishing direct contact, look for important signs such as:

— the nature of the response to your approach (was it cold and curt or friendly and co-operative?)
— the channels you have to go through before meeting a decision maker (are these formal and lengthy and designed to exert control or are they short and informal and designed for flexibility?)
— the amount of information given about likely vacancies and who makes the ultimate hiring decision.

You will be able to construct your own list of tell-tale signs.

Essentially these tell you something not only about an organisation's culture, but also about how hiring decisions are taken. In some cases, signs like these can combine to form a protective layer around an organisation which on the surface may appear to discourage direct approaches. This does not mean you will not be able to enter it. It just makes it that much more difficult and longer to achieve. Rather than making things harder for yourself, the trick is to focus your search on those organisations that are occasionally disposed to filling different levels of managerial and professional jobs from outside. In this situation you may find you are sacrificing a corporate climbing frame for an open structure that is adaptable, flexible and perhaps more creatively designed. It all depends on what you are looking for. In essence, you will need to judge it against your long term criterion; *what will this move do for my future employability?*

6

Plugging into Cyberspace: Interactive Job Hunting on the Internet

INTRODUCTION

If we accept the predictions, then the Internet could radically alter how we conduct our personal and professional lives. It is already seen as one of the most important developments of the twentieth century. It opens up information access and retrieval on such an unprecedented scale that many wonder how we ever managed without it. Over the next few years, as hundreds of satellites are launched to create an Internet in the sky, the Internet is set to transform markets, revolutionise the consumer process and influence our decision making through faster communication and more sophisticated information processing. Its changing technology is already affecting your ability to market yourself, to communicate and network with other people. It means you can turn your job hunting into a wholly interactive process between you and the recruiter, or you and your network contacts. By going online, you will be able to exchange information, brainstorm ideas and share common interests with fellow professionals. Using the Internet will enable you to find a job in much the same way as any other consumer process such as choosing a holiday, selecting a car or buying a house. All the signs are that in the next five years the Internet will become a vital advertising medium for employers and job hunters. Many feel it will overtake newspapers and journals, not only for jobs in IT but in most sectors of the labour market.

Large online recruitment databases are now commonplace. These give details of job listings and you can respond by sending your CV (there is often a small fee involved) as well as completing personal profile questionnaires. In future, you are more likely to be short listed as a result of placing your CV within a recruitment database than if you answer a newspaper advertisement. Initial screening and even screen-based interviewing are set to grow. These will affect not only how you match up to what recruiters want in terms of an 'ideal candidate', they will influence how you assess and respond to what is on offer in a labour market which, because of the facilities now on the Internet, will be far less fragmented and much easier to understand.

For managers and professionals with access to online technology, the whole pattern and process of job hunting is set to change. Through the Internet, you can already look for general job listings, for academic and professional posts, as well as recruitment agencies and selection consultants. If you want help with the design of your CV or in establishing a job search plan, or even background information on a targeted company, then this is a 'point and click' away. Not only can you do this in complete privacy; once you decide to go for an opening, you can then communicate with decision-makers direct, avoiding switchboards, secretaries and other intermediaries. In effect, the complicated business of bringing together buyers and sellers of labour will become much easier and far quicker.

THE 'NET', THE 'WEB' AND JOB HUNTING

Stretching back over 30 years, the Internet is now a global interactive computer network. As a public communications system, it means that anyone with a requisite computer, modem, telephone and Internet Service Provider (ISP) can use it. Predominantly based on e-mail or electronic mail, communication is cheap, usually highly reliable and very fast.

It is especially convenient because you can send the same message to several groups of people. E-mail now comprises over 80 per cent of Internet use, compared with 45 per cent for information searching. Public awareness of the Internet is steadily increasing in the UK. World wide, the Internet is expanding at an amazing rate. Vast numbers now plan to use it for personal communications, for marketing, on-demand information, and, most importantly for you, for electronic job hunting. A considerable array of new information services, including job search and advice, are now coming onto the Internet. These will make your research tasks easier and much more interesting.

Linked into the Internet is the World Wide Web (www), now shortened to the Web. You can visualise the Web as a 'sub-set' of information contained within the very much larger electronic base of the Internet. Think of the Web as the 'user friendly' face of the Internet. It makes information search and retrieval simpler and faster and it cuts out the need for you to have special computer skills and experience.

Each day it grows at an amazing rate, and its profile is continually altering. In mid-1997 it contained a 'guestimate' of something like 80 million pages, and a page is added every second! Apart from giving you information, the Web enables you to combine text, graphics, images and sound so that you can establish your own web page. It works through the use of 'browsers' such as Microsoft Explorer and Netscape. These retrieve the pages on which information is stored and then deliver these to your screen. Improvements in home page editors now make it far easier for you to establish your own personal site. You may wish to give this serious consideration as a valuable way of publicising yourself, especially if you are currently redundant.

Those familiar with computers will know there is nothing new in finding jobs online. What is new and important is the extent to which businesses and recruiters now use electronic information services. Already you can use the Internet to search for jobs on an international basis. Put into electronic form, news of vacancies and opportunities travels exceptionally fast. Those with the facilities to go online will therefore be at a distinct advantage in learning about these. Not only will you save time in tracking down an opening; you will also be able to tailor your search to what you want in the way of job, organisation, sector, location and even culture. Without the Internet, this would be difficult, lengthy and expensive.

WHAT'S NEEDED TO GO ONLINE

Here's a brief guide outlining what you will need in the way of equipment and software to go online. Much will hinge on your starting point – if you have an existing computer, whether you already know your way round the Internet. If you are buying new and starting from scratch, then your budget will be important. Take some specialised advice, see a system in operation, visit a cybercafe, and check out your subscription and telephone costs. Another suggestion is to visit a large university library and ask for some advice from a qualified information scientist. They may be able to give you some helpful tips.

Item One – a modem

This is a vital piece of equipment that connects your personal computer to a computer network through a telephone line. It comes with special communications software. This enables you to do different tasks such as sending and receiving faxes, setting up your PC as a voicemail answering machine, and accessing online networks. Because modems are rated by speed as well as data compression and error connection, faster usually means better. If you buy the fastest available, your calls will be cheaper and your waiting time to scan and download information will be much less.

Item Two – a printer

You will find a wide variety of inkjet and laser printers available. Quality, price, design and speed and whether you need colour will all need to be considered. Continual improvements now mean better value. Before you buy, see a demonstration to check print speeds and colour quality.

Item Three – a computer with CD-ROM and preferably a large monitor

Because you will need a CD-ROM drive, aim to buy the fastest you can afford, looking for twelve speed drives if you are buying from scratch. By opting for a 15″ or even 17″ high class monitor, you will see an considerable improvement when scanning the Internet. Other important components are the size of your hard drive, your random access memory (RAM), and your processor. Modern software is hungry for space, so aim to buy plenty of storage. From 1.6Gb to 2Gb should handle your current and future needs. In terms of RAM, because Internet software demands high speeds, you should install at least 16Mb or preferably 32Mb to make your operation go smoothly. Recent developments in processor speeds that support multimedia (MMX technology) are impressive and you should go for at least a 166 + MHz processor, upgradeable to 200MHz, if buying new.

Item Four – a telephone line

You will have to decide whether you want a separate line for your modem or whether you can manage on your existing line. Much will hinge on the number of users. With lots of incoming calls, you risk breaking your modem's connection.

Item Five – an Internet service provider

Besides buying the equipment, you will need to choose an Internet service provider (ISP). These are companies that provide the telephone connection to access the Internet. You have plenty to choose from and popular ones include LineOne (predominantly UK based), Compuserve, Pipex, Delphi, Demon, America Online, UK Online and MSN (Microsoft Network). All offer an array of different services: you can have online news, entertainment, reference sections, games and of course information retrieval via the Internet. Some now offer conferencing services and these can be valuable sources for networking and research. Be especially careful when choosing an ISP. This is because most of your Internet activities (Web page browsing, file downloading, e-mail transactions) will go through your ISP. Run a very strict check of their call rates and overall costs. Examine their software package to see if it supports your machine. Find out what support they give, if they provide advice and backup and whether they offer you Web space as part of their overall package. If in doubt seek advice, or contact a specialist at one of the Internet magazines, such as Internet Today. Before you sign your contract, thorough research of the market to find the best deals will certainly pay off.

Also check out what you need from your Web browser, which comes as part of the software from your ISP.This enables you to use the Web by navigating on a 'point and click' basis. Netscape and Internet Explorer from Microsoft are two standard browsing tools, which are continually updated and improved. If you have Windows 95 or later editions installed on your PC, you will already have your browser in situ. Should you need additional software, then you can find many free samples from online sources.

CHOOSING A SEARCH ENGINE

As a quick guide, try looking at some back numbers of the specialist Internet magazines already mentioned. These will give you plenty of information on getting connected as well as tips on searching through the maze of Web sites. To help you here, you will need to get to grips with a range of search engines. These are powerful tools, activated on a key word basis, which scan databases to find what you are looking for. Because they vary in size, structure and how they are designed and indexed, your choice of search engine can be quite critical, especially if you are in a hurry. Some search engines provide masses of information, but fail to be selective. You then spend far too much time discarding irrelevant data and far too little discovering what you really want to know. Choosing a search engine is often based on trial and error learning. Some are very high on quality and ease of access, others will be poor and time wasting. When you do locate a site that gives you what you need, save it in your Bookmark file for future reference. These can be organised so that they link in with different aspects of your job hunting. Examples of relevant search engines (there are hundreds of them on the Web) include Yahoo, Magellan, Alta Vista, SearchBank, Lycos, Infoseek, Web Crawler and Galaxy.

As well as specified search engines, you can use Global Search to find information on a specific topic. You can trawl through Yellow Pages for business listings, and access Newsgroups to engage in online discussion with fellow professionals. Specialist sites for professionals are growing in importance and you should find out what there is available in your own specialism. They now offer advice, assistance, keep you updated on professional matters and enable you to network quite effectively without leaving home.

World Wide Web sites have a prefix http://. Since some have a heavy graphics element to them, you can load them much faster if you turn off the Load Images option in your Web browser. During peak hours many access providers are overloaded and you have to wait or try again much later. This can be annoying and costly at times so pick the most cost effective time to browse and download.

VISITING USEFUL INTERNET SITES

Large numbers of pages are added to, and disappear from, the Internet every day. As such, it is not possible to give you a full listing of all the sites you can access in your job search. However, you will find these relevant and useful:

1. Career mosaic on http;//www.careermosaic-uk.co.uk — offers a career resource centre with plenty of advice on CVs, trends in careers and with extensive details of job listings, employment conditions and corporate develop-ments. You can download large amounts of information for your personal use.
2. IT Jobs on http://www.britain.eu.net/vendor/jobs/man-in.html — contains extensive, updated jobs listings
3. Monster Board on http;//www.monster.com/ — offers professional search facilities world-wide
4. Reed Personnel Services on http;//www.reed.pipex.com/reed/ — offers vacancy listings and applications
5. Virtual Headroom on http;//www.xmission.com/-wintrnx/virtual.html — details of CV posting and prices
6. Online Career Centre (OCC) Europe on http://www.occ,-coin/europe
7. World Careers Network (WCN) on http://www.wen-world.com
8. The Careers Services Unit (CSU) on http://www.pros-pects.csu.man.ac.uk — useful for recent graduates

The more you browse, the more sites you will find which fit your needs. Do be aware that much of the information on job hunting is geared to the American labour market. However, many more UK sites are about to emerge. You can always discard that which will not help you.

Another interesting way of finding opportunities is to visit the sites or 'home pages' of organisations which interest you. Virtually all large companies have established Web sites, often with employment sections which are easy to reach. It is less easy to find job listings or advertisements for small organisations with growth potential, though these may well have a Web site. Construct your own 'hit list' of likely employers, and then browse to see what is on offer from their jobs listings and advertised vacancies. If you don't see just what you are looking for, then scan for news on latest company news, initiatives, awards, contracts, results and product developments. Not only can you save these for future reference; they also offer pointers to future openings to fit your own skills and experience. Once you have pieced together your information, you may then consider that a direct approach to a named decision-maker will be advantageous. Sending your CV and other marketing literature has never been easier, quicker or less foolproof.

TIPS TO IMPROVE YOUR SEARCH EFFICIENCY

When you log on to the Internet, you are entering what can be called the world's largest library. Faced with such a vast and ever increasing information base, you may decide that it is far too costly and time consuming to find what you really need. However, help is at hand, and with a little planning and forethought you can soon become a competent searcher. Here are some general tips for you to follow:

■ As a beginner, select a simple word or term (eg career) and then try a number of search engines to see what comes up. You can then compare the quantity and quality of the 'hits' you have made and record which ones serve your needs best. Once you have done this several times you start to build up a feeling of which search engines are best for different purposes.

- Be very clear on what you are looking for, which may not always be easy, especially if you are just browsing. Try a combination of key words to see if you are being too narrow or too broad in your approach.
- Take advantage of the advanced facilities and special search methods within each search engine. You can then save the results and start building a dossier of advanced online search techniques. These will then be ready for use, on a 'horses for courses' basis for whatever kind of information you require.
- Try to avoid being side-tracked during your search. It is very easy to go into areas which interest you or seem fascinating, but it is your telephone bill that is mounting up. Choose times when costs are low and when search engines are not as crowded or overloaded. Happy surfing!

THE BENEFITS OF GOING ONLINE

As a beginner, you may find the Internet rather like a jungle, confusing and difficult to penetrate. Stick with it and you will soon find you can master the basics. As you progress you will be amazed at how many people will be prepared to share ideas and give information quite voluntarily and promptly. There are also many search engines that will act as your guide. Experiment with a number to see how far they help you with specific data. There is plenty of advice on different ways of searching, both screen-based and in a host of books and magazines of varying quality and detail. However, as with much information, this can soon go out of date.

Plugging into the Internet can deliver considerable benefits when it comes to job hunting.

- You have access to vast amounts of information, readily and speedily available and which would take you far longer to produce through conventional library search.

You can search databases, download files and scan current articles, news, reports, statistics, and opinions. What's more you can learn from large electronic libraries, track company data, and keep abreast of issues in your own field.

■ You can communicate and network with like-minded professionals through bulletin boards, e-mail, user groups and professional forums. You can join one of several thousand news groups in operation. Conferences and discussions are also at your disposal. Support groups for redundant professionals can be valuable in exchanging ideas, sharing experiences and picking up prospects.

■ You can find jobs listings by direct contact with selected organisations and specialist recruiters. Such listings give details of a wide range of specialised positions and forthcoming opportunities. You can see what is on offer, on a daily basis if necessary. Even when browsing, you may come across a position that whets your appetite. You can then respond quickly and positively.

■ If you are going for an interview, the Internet can assist you in your homework on the organisation and sometimes the job. Don't underestimate the impression which sound research can give to selectors.

Also at hand on the Internet is a rapidly developing range of career counselling services designed to increase your knowledge of yourself and where you want to go to. These services offer you the opportunity to use a wide variety of *career development tools*, usually on a fee-paying basis. The tools are designed to make you aware of choices and options, and are especially useful if you are considering a career change. They analyse what you already have to offer, often in terms of skills or personality. They also offer insights into your interests and where these may lead you.

Here are some examples:

Interest Inventories – these explore your vocational interests, temperaments and aptitudes

Personality questionnaires – these indicate how your personality influences your work preferences

Job Hunting Strategies – assistance with CV writing, interviewing skills, research techniques, networking

The trend towards managers and professionals using these services as part of an integrated approach to job hunting is set to develop. They can be particularly useful when you are unsure where you should be going and when you would like to explore different ideas, all from the comfort of your own home.

HOW RECRUITERS USE THE INTERNET

Finding the right people at the right price and time and in the right quantity has always posed a problem for recruiters, Traditional methods such as advertising, taking up unsolicited approaches, or relying on contacts and referrals all have their place. Nevertheless, many industries now face a severe shortage of skilled and highly qualified labour. Firms, especially those with global operations, are not only looking for relevant professional and technical expertise; they also want you to have a set of skills such as commercial awareness, team building in diverse cultures and a sound knowledge of information technology.

This is where *cyberspace recruiting* comes in and where you need to be familiar with its operation and what it means for your own job hunting. Just as all kinds of organisations now strive to stay abreast of developments in communications and technology, so you will need to know how to handle the Internet if you are to keep up with the game. Essentially, the Internet is changing the face of recruitment. It is saving time, paperwork and administrative support costs. By using a variety of electronic aids, recruiters can now widen their search activities, target more accurately and find the people they want faster and more cost effectively. These aids consist of:

■ *Electronic bulletin boards:* these are used to place messages to newsgroups, and enables them to give details of the organisation, its products and services, its recruitment policies and details of vacancies and potential openings. A comprehensive list of bulletin boards can be found on the *Internet*. They are also published regularly in Internet magazines such as *Internet* and *Internet Today*.

■ *E-mail:* this allows messages and information to be distributed world wide to reach vast numbers. Many data sources can now be accessed by e-mail: you just need the address and the directory. If you send your CV or complete an application form or standard personal profile, then e-mail is your main medium. Responses to your enquiry or application can be speedy and confidential.

■ *Electronic mailing lists:* these are similar to bulletin boards but far more open. Recruiters can use them to obtain information on issues of common interest within a particular topic area. Many professional organisations now have these. Recruiters who are also members of a profession (lawyers, engineers, accountants, architects, computer specialists etc) can receive the latest thinking and news from around the world. This enables them to capture and use information often critical to their daily operations.

Do not think these three aids are simply the preserve of recruiters. You can use them in the same way. For example, when you send your request to your selected list server (the computer programme that maintains the mailing list) you will also be able to send and receive messages from all subscribers on the list. By taking advantage of Internet technology, both you and recruiters will be able to interact with one another to an extent undreamed of even five years ago.

Recruiters are finding that the Internet is already delivering substantial benefits for themselves and for applicants, such as:

■ Online recruitment costs far less than traditional advertising. By taking the electronic route, recruiters can reach far more people on a global basis, almost at the touch of a button.

■ It allows recruiters to publicise their vacancies and opportunities in far more detail than is possible with traditional advertisements. Web pages can be designed to provide important additional data. By trawling, job hunters can look for information on rewards and recruitment and selection, product and service issues and even ideas on culture and goals.

■ It streamlines the recruitment process. Applicants can complete forms, personal profiles, and e-mail their CV. Applicant tracking systems can then match candidates to suitable vacancies, thus helping in compiling short lists and keeping candidates fully informed of their progress.

Some observers consider the rapid growth of electronic recruitment is so revolutionary that it will soon replace traditional recruitment practices. This is especially likely in global enterprises building sophisticated electronic networks to make a success of their international recruitment. Even in small and medium sized firms, relying on agencies, advertisements and search consultants may be too costly, slow and cumbersome, especially when they may be in a competition for only a handful of suitable candidates. In the next five years recruiters are clearly set to make much greater use of applicant tracking, screening and imaging devices as they strive to match new technology with their staffing needs.

Part Three:

Succeeding at the Selection Stage

$$\boxed{7}$$

Managing the Employment Interview: Putting on Your Best Performance

INTRODUCTION

Your interview performance will be a major factor in an employer's decision to accept or reject your application. While the employment interview is the most common method used (as well as misused) in employee selection, recent findings indicate that organisations are increasingly using a variety of other devices when selecting candidates for managerial and professional roles. For example: *Personality tests are standard practice in up to 37 per cent of organisations; Cognitive tests are common in up to 41 per cent of organisations; Assessment or development centres are used in up to 24 per cent of organisations.*

Nevertheless, you are unlikely to be offered a position (be it a job, an opportunity or career opening) in the current job market without undergoing one or indeed several interviews. Multiple interviews are rapidly becoming the norm rather than the exception, especially if you are seeking middle or senior managerial positions.

A typical format, which you are highly likely to encounter, could be as follows:

■ An initial screening interview, often short in duration,

conducted by perhaps a personnel specialist or a search and selection consultant, or an employment agency.

■ A second interview, going into more depth, often with a more senior person at line management or board level.

■ A final interview, perhaps with a panel, or a very senior member of the organisation (MD, Chief Executive, Vice-President, Chairman).

Clearly much will depend on the seniority of the position, the selection methods of the organisation, and the importance attaching to the job. Whatever format it takes, you will find that each interview will differ in focus, in the topics covered, in the way you are evaluated and in the quality of the interviewer. Your preparation and performance therefore needs to mirror these differences. Reaching the short list is a major achievement in itself, given the highly competitive nature of job search within professional and managerial markets. However, since the really crucial stage lies ahead, the significance of the job interview for your future career success cannot be overemphasised.

Whatever stage you are at in your career development, you should view the employment interview as *a game of high stakes*. You may see it as an opportunity to:

■ develop your skills and reputation by joining a highly prestigious employer;

■ re-enter the job market after redundancy; or change career direction and interests;

■ move into a more senior position, or progress more quickly in your chosen field;

■ broaden your experience or undertake an interesting project or assignment.

Much will hinge on how you perform and because of this most job hunters regard the interview as the most difficult aspect of their programme. You may be lacking in recent interview experience, or over anxious about the outcome, or you may fear rejection. Alternatively you may be elated at the prospect of performing, delighted to be given an opportunity to extol your virtues and confident about the outcome because of your competencies and personality.

Whatever your feelings and aspirations, it may be sensible at the outset to reflect on some of the shortcomings of employment interviews. These are likely to give you a greater insight into how your performance may be judged or how you might wish to prepare to bring about a positive outcome.

- Despite recent improvements in design and methods of evaluation, the interview is still regarded as somewhat ineffective in predicting future job performance. Inter-viewers may make snap decisions based on false assumptions and instinct, rather than careful analysis and rational thought.
- The event can be very elusive for both interviewer and interviewee. Making sure you have a complete record of what goes on, evaluating the impact of both sides on one another, assessing how much of the decision is based on first impressions or bias – all these tend to cloud the final outcome.
- Your non-verbal behaviour, interpersonal skills, likeability, attractiveness and your ability to make a good first impression are likely to be weighed far more heavily than your recent work experience, level of education, hard earned qualifications and the ways you fit the job specification.
- Many interviewers are just not up to the job. They wrongly believe they have the perceptive ability and data processing skills to select the best candidate. Stereotyping, weighing negative information more highly than positive information, and coming to a conclusion within the first few minutes all make for poor decision making and the selection of the wrong person. For you, this can be frustrating.

After all this, you may well despair of a fair and objective interview, feel the whole process is some kind of lottery, with luck, chance and bias all affecting your ability to perform well in what is essentially a rather false situation. The short answer is *don't*. For, while the interview has its undoubted short-comings (and it can never be seen as a perfect selection device), it does have some considerable advantages which you should take into account in your preparations. Let us look at some of these in more detail.

1. It enables selectors to see a candidate 'in the flesh'. The face to face meeting can be a very good way of drawing together different pieces of information in order to establish a clearer picture of your suitability as a candidate. The idea of personal chemistry between interviewer and interviewee is often critical, especially if they are to work closely together or be part of a diverse and multi-skilled team. Chemistry, or lack of it, is also cited as a reason for dispensing with the services of an employee, particularly at a senior strategic level. Therefore, carefully appraise how you can project your own personality and interpersonal skills in order to heighten your attractiveness and likeability in this important area.

2. Interviews can be valuable in assessing your level of motivation, or your commitment and enthusiasm to join a particular organisation. These are often important issues when an interviewer is trying to establish if you are likely to fit in with colleagues at different levels. Indeed, the concept of 'fit' into an organisation's culture can be uppermost in the mind of both interviewer and interviewee. Here you can be rated on such issues as personal values (pacifists don't really fit into military establishments), management style (dictators may fail to fit into an empowerment culture), dress and appearance (important in customer-facing, persuasive and interpersonal roles). Also, you may just be compared with other people in the team or, if they want drastic changes in the prevailing culture, they will want to know how you will contribute to this. The tactic here is not only to consider how you are seen as suitable for the position. Just as important is how you see yourself in terms of 'fit'. By carefully drawing up what you want from a prevailing culture or work environment, you

are far less likely to make a mistake. Better to endeavour to know at the outset if it is not right for you than to accept and then find it has been a very costly mistake.

3. Finally, it gives you the opportunity to find out far more about what the job entails. Hopefully, you can explore the openings or opportunities which may exist, the ways in which your performance may be judged, as well as any training and personal development prospects. Rewards, promotion, benefits, contractual issues, working conditions, political insights and what is really expected of you are all matters which need to be established at some stage. The interview is a very appropriate setting for these. Above all, the interview is important from your point of view because it can provide a forum for detailed negotiation on terms and conditions of employment before you enter into a contract. Afterwards it may be too late, especially if you are considering golden handshakes or severance settlements.

COPING WITH DIFFERENT FORMS OF INTERVIEW

Let us now assess four kinds of interview that you are likely to encounter in your job hunting.

Situational interviews

These are designed around a number of questions which focus on situations which might happen in a job. You, the applicant, are then asked what you would do in such a situation. In essence you are presented with a series of hypothetical questions which are very future oriented and which tend to test your powers of imagination. The attention of the interviewer is far less on your actual job experience. Taking this approach is most appropriate with recent graduates, post-graduates or those who have just completed a training course. Behind the questioning lies a desire to find out your potential to learn and perform well in the future, as well as your interpersonal and communication skills. Panel interviews, often encountered when you are applying for positions in the public sector, are particularly fond of asking such questions and they can come in various forms; for example:

- If you were to be appointed to this post, what changes would you wish to make to current staffing levels and how would you assess the implications of your decision? (A two part question, with a sting in the tail!)
- Imagine you are confronted with a major downturn in business in your division and you have to come up with new product ideas very quickly; on what bases would you make your decisions?
- What would you do if after your first month here, your supervisor feels you are not pulling your weight in the team; how would you respond to such criticism?

How will your responses to such questions be evaluated? In the main, they will be based on the traits or features seen as important in future job performance, eg your level of creativity, your adaptability and flexibility, your flair for innovation and your ability to harness a small number of key points into a coherent and persuasive answer. Keep your replies concise and relevant; don't ramble.

Behaviour description interviews (often referred to as experience based)

These are concerned with your past performance and behaviour and how you coped in different situations in your previous role or activity. The emphasis is very much on your previous job experience and how it relates to the opening for which you are being considered. The search is on here to see if you can *hit the ground running*, ie are you up to speed as well as up to all parts of the job. Attention will also centre around how much additional training or development you may need and if, having done the job already, you can now do it all over again in a new context. While the emphasis is on gathering information which is 'past-oriented', nevertheless, the interviewer is endeavouring to use what is gleaned to predict how you will perform in similar situations in the future, and to compare you with other successful employees. Much of the rationale for this approach is based on the notion that 'the best predictor of future performance is past performance'. Questions may be more difficult to predict when you are confronted with this type of interview. That said, you will find yourself being asked to describe previous jobs in detail, including achievements, responsibilities, failures and successes, as well as what you enjoy and don't enjoy. For those in transition after redundancy there is often a sharp focus on what happened in your last position. Your preparations should bear these important issues in mind, since more and more organisations are moving towards this form of interview for candidates with relevant work experience.

Here are three sample questions:

1. Talk me through an occasion when you successfully dealt with an angry but important client.
2. Give me an example when you failed to meet an important deadline and what happened.
3. When you were in industrial relations, how did you cope with the stress of industrial conflict?

This kind of interview tends to be highly structured and you can easily recognise it from the style of the questions. Emphasis is placed on an analysis of the job in question. From this certain questions are then formulated and these often follow a format such as job knowledge; job simulation; qualifications and credentials necessary to perform the job. Finally, you will be asked how you handle certain situations such as conflict, low productivity and morale, high turnover and absenteeism, or dealing with people who resist change measures. Each candidate is usually asked the same questions, often in the same order: a scoring scheme is devised and answers are recorded and rated. Those with the highest scores are usually then selected.

What can we say about these types of interview? They are tough, they need very careful preparation and they dwell on both your strengths and weaknesses. So, what can you do about them?

Here are four suggestions which will aid your preparation.

1. Thoroughly evaluate each aspect of your recent experience in terms of both accomplishments and benefits. Quantify wherever possible, showing targets met and exceeded and how you came to perform well. At the same time make a list of examples of where things didn't go to plan and why.

2. Prepare a portfolio of examples of projects undertaken, teams worked in, assignments completed, and relate these specifically to the job for which you are being considered. Always give your best example, though this may not be easy when you are under pressure.

3. Break down your current or last job(s) into its component parts, highlighting where there is a fit with the new job you have in mind. Highlight special attributes or skills used and the lessons you have learned in both a technical or managerial sense, as well as interpersonal and problem-solving issues. Continually rehearse these until you are fluent in recall and in the speed of your response. While some pauses are very useful in giving you time to structure your reply, consistent hesitation is damaging to your prospects. Memorising key words can trigger your memory.

4. Consistently analyse what skills were used in what tasks and then prepare a set of strong visual images which show how your skills and experience can be effectively transferred into this new job. Put across your message that your readily transferable skills will bring tangible benefits to your prospective employer.

Unstructured interviews

In sharp contrast to the two examples above, these do not have any predetermined structure. Instead, they are loosely organised and with no predetermined rules. Discussion is often wide-ranging, with the focus shifting on those issues which may hold the interest of the interviewer, or on those which may give some indication of future job performance. In many cases, it is the least satisfactory in terms of predicting how a candidate will perform. Also, it is open to substantial criticism in terms of unfair or biased questioning. Yet, this type of interview is very common and, more importantly, is highly unreliable. As a candidate, if you encounter such an interview, then you will need to find out three key issues should you be rejected, preferably by going back to the interviewer after a short interval and enquiring:

- how you performed overall and in relation to other candidates who might be considered;
- what aspects of your performance tended to be weighted more highly than others;
- what can you learn to enable you to perform better next time.

Such an interview format makes it difficult to elicit relevant information from you as an interviewee. The interviewer may ask a series of leading or closed questions and these may be upsetting, unfair and negative, thereby failing to give you the opportunity to extol your achievements and potential. Just as important is that this type of interview is unlikely to give you the opportunity to learn about the real demands of the job. It won't tell you about the expectations of future colleagues, or the level of support you might expect, or whether the job is the right one for you. For better or worse, we are stuck with it. Treat it with some care — the interviewer may not have a clue what to look for!

However, you can enhance your chances of success if you:

1.   Carefully prepare in advance a number of key features (say

five or six) of your application which you want to establish as your USPs (unique selling points). Construct a short resume of these and thoroughly rehearse them, out loud, until you can recall them quickly. Then think of the opportunities you may have to present these to the interviewer; in opening remarks, in pauses, in linking one theme to another, in summarising at the end of the interview.

2. Keep your responses short and very much to the point. Replies of about four sentences often achieve much higher impact than long and rambling responses which are irrelevant and boring.

Look for signs of interest as well as indifference through eye contact and body language. While you may not control the structure of the interview, you can influence its content. In this type of interview more weight is likely to be given to two things: *how you say things rather that what is said (tone, emphasis, accent, pitch, volume, fluency) and the impression you make through your non-verbal behaviour, often in the first few minutes.*

Panel interviews

These tend to consist of between three and five members, often drawn from different parts of an organisation and may include an independent assessor. In some cases panels have been known to comprise over 50 members, particularly when a very senior appointment is being made. In this case, it appears everyone wants to get in on the act! This type of interview is very common when applying for posts in public sector bodies (health service, local government, civil service). Panels are often designed to make quite rapid decisions (frequently on the day of the interview), as well as giving a number of people a stake in the decision making. They are often seen as guardians of fairness and equity and may consist of someone representing the interests of equal opportunities. In addition they can be helpful in overcoming bias or nepotism.They can also help in establishing accountability and distributing responsibility.

That said, do be aware that they also have some serious shortcomings and an appreciation of these will help you to prepare more effectively for this type of interview.

- Facing a panel, especially if you have only had experience of one-to-one interviews, can be like being asked 'when did you last see your father?' — a form of interrogation or even judgement. Their very formality (you may be given an allotted time of perhaps 30–35 minutes) may make it difficult for you to relax and establish an early rapport with all members.

- Rather than being a conversation with a purpose, which is the basis of most interviews, panels may be inflexible and somewhat rigid in approach; questions are fired at you, often with little relationship to each other, since they reflect the particular interests of members. Some superficial, even irrelevant, questions can emerge, often from lay members with pet interests, which may upset your train of thought and level of concentration.

- It is unlikely you will be able to answer questions in any depth and you may find you provide quite short responses to important issues which require more detail or level of analysis. It is very easy in these circumstances to give a poor reply and then let this affect the rest of your performance. Just try to forget the last reply and focus on improving your next one.

- In some cases, but thankfully for you there are not too many of these, the panel can behave like a competitive group, with little control by the chairman. This can inhibit you as a candidate, and you will lose the opportunity to be spontaneous and flexible. In such cases, sit tight and let it ride over you.

You may also find two other features of panel interviews to be important in your preparations. First, they may be supplemented by a series of psychometric tests, the results of which could be available to some panel members, and you may also be asked to make a short presentation (about ten minutes or so) on a previously agreed topic. Secondly, prior to a panel interview (which may be held in the afternoon) you may be invited to a reception or buffet, where other members of the organisation may be gathered. Don't underestimate this event, since evaluation and feedback may be given to panel members. This approach has different titles – trial by sherry, assessment by knife and fork; you may well have your own name for it. As a serious candidate, this can be a golden opportunity to use your interpersonal, communication and questioning skills to good effect in order to find out more about the job, while continuing the process of impression management.

What can you do to improve your chances here? Consider these as helpful suggestions:

1. Endeavour to make an impression on all members through the judicious use of head movements and eye contact with each questioner, then scanning the others to reinforce your message. Be aware of the body language of panel members, from nods and glances, smiles and posture shifts.
2. Pay very special attention to answering technical or strategic questions from experts on the panel. Also focus on what might be simple or naïve questions from other members and answer these with the same assurance and focus. Endeavour to compile a number of creative ideas which could form the basis of discussion while at the same time ensuring you have up your sleeve a set of searching questions for the panel to consider. Remember that selection on this basis is very much one of consensus and it does not pay to alienate those whom you may not meet again, even after appointment.
3. Panel members are just as susceptible to first impressions, and their decisions will be both subjective and objective. Establish an early rapport by relaxing and opening up quickly to the questions. At the same time try to achieve some kind of balance in the interview between talking and listening. A ratio of 80/20 or 70/30 between candidate and panel members should be aimed at but if the panel wish to talk more than you, then settle down and rely on your impression management skills.

INTERVIEWERS AND THEIR QUESTIONS

There is now very substantial evidence that the selection process, especially for managerial and professional groups, is becoming longer and more rigorous. Several factors are contributing to these trends and it is important for you to appreciate these, since they will affect both your style of preparation and your attitude and motivation to job search.

Increasingly organisations are becoming far more conscious of the need to select high quality candidates at all levels in order to maintain their competitive advantage. Since the costs of taking on poor quality staff and then subsequently dispensing with their services are now very high, mistakes at the selection stage have to be avoided wherever possible. Hence there is increased emphasis on improving the format of the employment interview and the use of additional measures such as psychometric tests, assessment centres and biodata.

Major changes in their structure, markets and technologies across all kinds of organisations have meant a change of focus on the competencies and attitudes of applicants. You are now highly likely to be rigorously assessed not only on your existing skills and experience but also on what you can contribute in the future. Can you clearly demonstrate how flexible and adaptable you are; do you have the drive to be part of a major culture-change exercise; are you more creative and able to cope better with uncertainty and turbulence than the next candidate? If these seem very tall orders, and they certainly are, then by being aware of these trends and expectations, at least you are part of the way towards accomplishing them.

Clearly the agenda has changed and will continue to change as more organisations come to resemble loose teams of workers coming together to work on a particular project, before disbanding and then moving on to another one. This will seriously affect employer and employee relations and you are likely to see major changes in the psychological contract which you have with your employer. Interviewers will face a heavy burden of responsibility in trying 'to get things right first time', and this is likely to be shown not only in how they design the interview but also how they approach prospective candidates such as yourself. While selection becomes more stringent, high calibre candidates will be able to negotiate more rewarding positions as the pool of scarce skills diminishes.

Where then does this leave interviewers and their approach to the selection of *you* as a candidate? Several issues can be discerned here.

Pressure on interviewers is likely to increase. The costs and implications of making a wrong decision will become more visible and measurable. Greater care in processing your application and devising a more structured interview based on your past experience or future potential will be much more in evidence. This will be of distinct benefit to those who prepare fully and are not judged predominantly on first impressions and likeability.

Greater use will be made of the information you provide before you attend for interview. Pre-screening of such material as your CV, application form, personal portfolio, references, covering letters and any telephone conversations or earlier contacts is likely to be more rigorous. By giving very careful attention to this kind of information you will be able to influence the eventual outcome of the interview. It is well known that before you arrive for interview, the interviewer will have formed a picture or image of you and your fitness for the opening. Then in the first part of the discussion, the interviewer will closely compare your actual behaviour with the image formed earlier, and frequently make a decision, after a very short period of time, of reject or accept. As the saying goes, *'you've only got four minutes'*.

HANDLING DIFFERENT TYPES OF QUESTIONS

Let us turn now to the type of questions you are likely to encounter, and how you can construct responses which will give not only a good impression but also illustrate your skills and suitability.

Questions are the building blocks of the interview which overwhelmingly consists of talk, followed by a decision. The quality and phrasing of questions and how well these will elicit information from you as a candidate will clearly affect the outcome of the encounter. You may already have suffered at the hands of interviewers who give you little opportunity to shine simply because they ask the wrong questions which have little to do with job relatedness. What then can you expect?

Leading questions

These are very one-sided and betray specific attitudes of the questioner. They tend to have very little value in eliciting quality information and essentially feed what the interviewer wants to hear. By prompting you to give a desired answer, the interviewer is giving you no opportunity to show your problem solving skills or your depth of experience. Here are two examples:

'Presumably you found your last position failed to meet your high expectations?'

'Would you agree with me that leaders are always born and certainly not made?'

From even this small sample you will appreciate that the interviewer will learn nothing from your response and you will find it difficult to give information in return. Try to turn the question round to provide an opportunity to put your main points across: for example:

'What has attracted me to this position is that your organisation expects high standards of its staff and my own approach to work is to continually strive to improve my own and my team's performance.'

Closed questions

Often used by interviewers who want precise and factual information to confirm that previously conveyed in CVs and application forms. Responses are usually on a yes/no basis, and while they give the interviewer the ability to control the answer, they are very boring to deal with and candidates can soon lose interest. Here are two examples:

'What was the class of degree you obtained from university?'
'Did you go straight from school into your current company?'

Probing questions

Where an interviewer feels a candidate may be concealing vital information, then probing questions may start to be asked. For example, in relation to the standard of education reached; or qualifications obtained, or the truthfulness of your actual work experience; or about gaps in your previous employment. Candidates may try to hide or gloss over some aspects of their career history which, in their opinion, may be seen as something the interviewer should not know about. There is always a danger that this will eventually be extracted from you and this can affect perceptions of your openness and truthfulness. Here are three examples:

'I see you quickly parted with your last company but you are reluctant to say why, so tell me.'
'I understand you were in that department but you have still not told me what position you held.'
'I need to know what precisely happened when you were moved from sales into operations.'

Probing questions are used far more extensively in interviews for senior professional and managerial positions, particularly when the strategic importance of the position will affect the organisations' future. The reason for this is that interviewers will have built up a set of expectations of the 'ideal candidate'. They will frequently base their decisions on how they expect interviewees to perform in the interview. Such expectations will become even more important when the interviewer has accumulated only limited information on your track record, your level of performance, your skills and experience, and how effective you will be in making the transition to this level of responsibility. Clearly there is a risk factor operating here and if the interviewer is somewhat risk-aversive, then more information and examples of appropriate behaviour will be sought by means of probing questions. Be fully prepared for this approach, remembering that its often the supplementary questions which pose the most difficulty. Think very carefully about how you might tackle the following questions which are very future-oriented but which focus on the kind of expectations the interviewer will have in mind for senior positions.

- Provide me with concrete evidence that you can build and manage teams.
- How do you adapt to rapidly changing and often difficult situations?
- In what ways do you resolve complex problems?
- By what means will you encourage innovation and stimulate creativity?
- How will you communicate your vision of the future to your senior management team?

Open questions

These are used to establish rapport, to set you at ease, to explore opinions and attitudes and to encourage you to be open and informative, while feeling at ease and relaxed. Their main purpose is two-fold; to enable you to give much more detail than in closed questions, and, more importantly, to give you the chance to select relevant points, order your responses and illuminate with examples and ideas. While they may appear quite simple on the surface, open questions are capable of being answered at different levels and with different emphasis and style. Try these as examples by devising three ways of answering them and then asking someone to evaluate your responses.

1. Shall we begin our discussion by you telling me about yourself?
2. What are your thoughts on the distinction between leadership and management?
3. If an employee came to discuss a personal problem, what would you do?

While these may be regarded as standard questions, it is worth making the point that in many behaviour or experienced-based interviews, you may not be asked such general questions at all. Instead you may be immediately plunged into answering questions which are specifically related to the skills and characteristics of the job you applied for. These can be followed up with a wide range of supplementaries which probe deeper and deeper. Here is one as an example:

■ What kind of pressure are you under at the moment?
■ Yes, I see you have tight monthly deadlines, but how do you cope with them?
■ Yes, I appreciate that much will depend on your own time management skills, but give me two examples of these which you find beneficial and actually work.
■ Quite so, but now tell me about the deadlines you have missed.
■ What kind of repercussions occurred when your boss found out?
■ How did you ensure such a problem did not arise again?
■ On reflection, in what other ways could you have handled the situation?

The form and style of questions, and the ways in which you interpret and respond to them, are a vital part of the process by which the interviewer builds up a picture of your suitability. You may find the following suggestions will help to improve your performance:

■ Select a number of questions which you feel will be asked at the interview, then construct three replies which highlight different approaches to answering each question. Compare and contrast these and note how far they are effective in coming to the point quickly, in conciseness and in relevance.

■ With the help of a partner or friend, design a mock interview of 30–35 minutes; prepare about 25 to 30 standard questions about your background, work experience, skills and career development and then record your performance by video recorder. Play it back and be your own worst critic. If you are not satisfied, then repeat the exercise until you are performing well.

■ Think carefully about how well you are communicating and persuading. Check if your body language, voice, tone, pitch, accent and use of pauses and silence is conveying the message which the interviewer wishes to receive. To obtain feedback on this, ask colleagues, friends, partners, about their expectations of you and what aspects are likely to enhance or impede you at interview.

Finally in this section on interview questions, here are two very common questions with a suggested scoring criteria for the replies:

1. How would you seek the views of your subordinates when trying to improve the daily operations of the business?

    Good (3)   Answer characterised by active consultation and involvement with all subordinates; examples could include quality circles, empowerment, suggestion schemes, delegation, brainstorming techniques, problem solving activities, regular meetings and other strategies, all designed to encourage positive and constructive feedback and participation.

    Fair (2)   Answer limited to a 'wait and see if a particular problem arises' and then seeking subordinate views. This is essentially a reactive approach, though some of the methods above could be used.

    Poor (0)   Answer characterised by the candidate failing to understand why subordinate involvement was of any value. Managers operating on a 'tell, do' system tend to take this approach.

2. Would you like to begin by telling me a little about yourself?

   Good (3) Answer characterised by focusing on those issues of personality, skills or experience which relate to the job and to the means by which performance in the job will be evaluated; capacity to grow and to meet future expectations, dependability and conscientiousness, managerial style, career goals and aspirations.

   Fair (2) Answer characterised by partial selection of some of these points but failing to link these to what is required for successful job performance now and in the future.

   Poor (0) Answer characterised by a lengthy account of your childhood, schools, family, friends, hobbies, interests, out of work activities. In one known case, a candidate talked about all these issues for 45 minutes without pausing before the interviewer was able to change the topic!

The effective answer is one which addresses the key issues posed in the question and gives interviewers what they expect or want to hear. Your personal opinion may not always be valued, unless specifically asked for.

EFFECTIVE LISTENING AND QUESTIONING

Candidates consistently let themselves down at interview because they are far more concerned with putting across their message than with using their listening skills to build up rapport and influence the outcome. All too often a candidate will go to considerable lengths to prepare and rehearse a series of well structured and sound replies to standard interview questions. This is not to deny the importance of such an approach. Indeed, it will add to your confidence to do this as part of your own preparation. However, there is another aspect of the influencing process, and that is through active listening, more commonly referred to as attentive behaviour skills.

Before analysing these, consider for a moment some of the factors which might affect how well you listen and understand at an interview, and then assess how you may tackle the problem.

■ The interviewer gives the immediate impression of being cold, impersonal, lacking in empathy and unimpressed with your application. You respond by being defensive, by failing to open up and give a good account of your experience and suitability. You withdraw your enthusiasm and energy. You become far less concerned with the questions and instead go through the motions of providing standard or inappropriate answers.

■ You are feeling anxious and apprehensive because of your lack of recent interview experience, and with each answer you become more self-conscious and unsure of yourself. Your concentration goes, your mind becomes blank and the sound responses of which you are capable just do not flow. You may well ramble, or say one thing, but mean another. You may also give one poor reply and then let this affect the rest of the interview.

■ You have concentrated so hard on your impression management skills that you neglect the importance of listening to the interviewer. This results in talking at the interviewer rather than establishing early rapport and evaluating important cues and nuances. Expressions of interest or boredom with your replies, combined with verbal clues as to how you are progressing, may all be missed because you are not actively listening. Above all, you just do not answer the questions, and this is one of the most important factors cited by interviewers in rejecting candidates.

How then can you improve your attentive behaviour so that you clearly demonstrate to the interviewer that you are actively listening, while at the same time improving your prospects of being selected? Several techniques are at your disposal.

1. Pay particular attention to your body language (essentially a counterpart of verbal language) in the form of an upright and alert posture, leaning forward at moments of special interest, moving position when topics change, using gestures to emphasise key points, nodding slightly when in agreement. Minimal eye contact often creates the impression of low energy levels, lack of self confidence, shyness and modesty. These are hardly prerequisites for a professional or managerial role!

2. Use reinforcing words such as:
    'I understand that and feel it is important ...';
    'Yes, that is how I often feel about that particular issue...';
    'I fully appreciate it can be difficult but I have found that...'

    These give the impression that you are following the argument, that you are tuned to the direction it is taking and that you have a contribution to make.

What you need to avoid in the interview is any behaviour which can be seen as non-attentive; for example, yawning, looking at the floor or out of the window, finger tapping and hand wringing, inspecting your fingernails, infrequent eye contact, and monosyllabic answers. All these effectively destroy the rapport which you should be endeavouring to establish within the interview.

Your questioning skills will often form part of the expectations of the interviewer. If these are not of the standard normally associated with candidates for a particular position, then you are likely to be seen as someone who has not prepared fully, is not motivated to do the job and may not fit into the new team or work culture. From your point of view, the answers to your questions will form a vital part of your perception of the position. Here are some probing questions to ask of yourself:

Is it really what you are looking for and does it fit into your overall career aspirations?

Do you know enough about the culture of the organisation to make a successful transition?

Are there aspects of the job which are least satisfying and perhaps even unacceptable?

Are the prospects longer term or is this simply a sideways move with a fancy title?

Are you expected to perform at a much higher level than you are doing at the moment?

You can easily construct a series of important issues on which you seek information and clarification. However, you will not find acceptable answers to all these at the interview, especially if it is a preliminary one, and in some cases you will have to take things on trust. In the same way that you may be judged by what appears 'on the surface', so you too will have to weigh what you do know about the job with what you would really like to know. In some interviews, you can come away with far less information than you would have wished, especially if you have not seized the opportunity to ask relevant questions.

Endeavour to compile a list of critical questions about features of the position which you feel are especially important. These will obviously vary according to your aspirations and circumstances, but here are a few ideas which you may find of value:

■ What do you need to know in making an effective transition into this new role? Here you should think about how your goals and attitudes will change, how it will affect your personal development, what will be the impact on your personal life, how will it shape your identity, what changes will there be to your daily routine, what kind of team will you be joining and how will you be viewed. Construct your questions around some of these and ask them when invited, especially if the interview fails to give you the answers you are looking for. Don't neglect the political dimension of any job; sound awareness of this is even more important when designing your questions.

Learn the ropes, especially at strategic level, or you may face the prospect of being asked to leave.

■ Is the position likely to give me job satisfaction? Here you should try and ascertain how far it will enable you to develop your talents even further. Will it stretch and extend you without too much adverse stress; are you going to achieve something worthwhile? Is it a role which has prestige and recognition and does it provide challenge and variety and autonomy? Is it reasonably secure given the current climate; will it lead to something better? Are the working conditions conducive to good performance; are the rewards fair and equitable; will your interest soon wane? If you have your own special needs or agenda, try to identify how far these will be met in the position.

■ In what ways will your performance be evaluated and by whom? Here you need to ascertain if the organisation undertakes regular performance appraisal, the ways in which this is carried out, the degree of training and supervision you may expect. Also find out how far you will have to carry out your own self-development, what happens if you don't come up to expectations, the likely compensation package which will be given if you are asked to part company, the policy of the organisation on redundancy and support given if this occurs. Again, find out about the reporting procedures for the job in question and to whom you are directly accountable. Define what to you are the critical areas here and then construct your questions accordingly. By doing so, you may well avoid problems and misunderstandings at a later date. Ensuring you know how you will receive feedback on your performance in this new role is a vital part of your interview questioning. Don't neglect it, especially if the job is highly visible and accountable and the culture is one of 'hiring and firing'. If several recent departures have hit the headlines, be especially wary.

MANAGING THE FIRST FOUR MINUTES

There is substantial evidence that interviewers display idiosyncratic interview techniques, weigh responses in very different ways and come to very different conclusions about the same candidate. Small wonder that you may think all your detailed and careful preparation may be a waste of time and that being yourself is the best strategy. Unfortunately this is not an effective approach, and what you need to be aware of is that the employment interview is essentially *reactive in nature; in other words both sides involved affect each other's behaviour and much of this is affected by bias.*

We have already suggested your previous data will have established certain expectations in the mind of the interviewer before you actually meet. One of the idiosyncrasies of the interview process is that very many interviewers make a decision to accept or reject your application within the first four minutes of meeting you. They then spend the rest of the interview looking for information which supports that decision. In effect, that decision is very likely to be based on their immediate perceptions of you and how far you fit their own picture of 'you within the actual job'. At the same time you will have formed certain impressions of your own about the job and the organisation and will then spend the interview deciding whether or not you want the job if it is offered. Some findings indicate that interviewers will make a judgement on very small samples of your behaviour and 80 per cent of these relate to your appearance and body language. They may well be seen as surface impressions rather than judgements, but the important point is *they stick!*

Let us examine what is likely to occur in the first four minutes, and what can be seen as critical behaviour on your part. In your first four minutes, you will go through several stages, all of which are opportunities for you and the interviewer to make inferences and interpretations.

Stage 1 Exchanging introductions and pleasantries: hand-shakes, the first direct eye contact; entering the interview setting, with awareness of its formality, decor, comfort, design, noise, spatial layout. Sitting down, establishing a positive posture; use of body language, smiles, gaze: this first stage of establishing rapport is most important in enabling you to cooperate and open up to subsequent questions. Rapport also involves trust and relaxation on both sides and provides the background against which you will endeavour to rapidly build a social relationship. It will be affected by the friendliness of the interviewer, the warmth of the welcome, the style of greeting, the ice-breaking techniques used and the general air of cordiality which surrounds the occasion. You can affect rapport and make the interviewer feel this is going to be an enjoyable discussion not only by your responses, but by your presence, appearance and level of enthusiasm.

Stage 2 The interviewer will (hopefully) go through the format of the interview, establishing its structure and possible timing; this may be followed by a description of the job and the organisation. This is where you use your listening skills and body language.

Stage 3 It is likely that your application, and the data you have already supplied, will be checked and this then leaves the ground clear to begin the question and answer session, which comprises the bulk of the interview.

Stage 4 Opening questions and responses; perhaps there is only time for one or two before the first four minutes is up. At this stage, both sides have entered the important area of seeking and interpreting information and reaching conclusions. Little hard data has been given, yet impressions have been formed and are highly likely to remain.

You may rightly ask therefore, just how have I been judged and what can I do to improve?

Essentially you have just been through four minutes of limited verbal behaviour. At the same time you have given off non-verbal behaviour in the form of style, dress, mannerisms, tone of voice, accent, stance and personal attractiveness. Both you and the interviewer have presented a social face to each other, while constantly monitoring each other's performance. If you are judged within the first four minutes, then it is highly likely the interviewer was unduly influenced not only by your non-verbal behaviour but also by your personality. You have presented yourself rather like a book and you have been evaluated on the basis of your 'cover'. Here are four factors that clearly affect the judgement of the interviewer. They also enable you to present positive non-verbal signals which will significantly enhance your prospects:

Your appearance – is it relevant for the position? Does it convey an image of confidence, alertness. Is there anything that might give the impression you are not fitted for the job?

Your face – are you displaying warmth with your smile? Is your use of eyebrows, lips, frowns, eye movements and gaze pattern making an impact?

Your body posture – are you focused and attentive, or slouching and diffident? Are you mirroring the interviewer's body language? Do you co-ordinate your gestures and movements?

Your paralanguage – how do you say things in terms of pitch, tone, speed, accent, and stress on certain words, use of certain phrases?

Throughout the first four minutes interviewers may well be looking for qualities that they prefer. The process of measuring you against other candidates is frequently impressionistic and subjective; in a word it is biased! What can you do to offset such bias?

■ First, be aware that bias exists in several forms. Thus carefully evaluate which aspects of your application and performance could lead to bias and try to correct them where possible.

■ Secondly, try especially hard to create a picture of competence and similarity of attitude with the interviewer.

■ Thirdly, make the interviewer aware of your familiarity with the key components of the job. Even on small samples of what you say or do, the interviewer will form an impression of your reliability and sound acquaintance with the job. Again consider how you can quickly create the impression not only that you can do the job but are also motivated to do it and keen to join the organisation.

It is by becoming more aware of the interviewer's feelings, thoughts, intentions and actions that you can begin to effectively influence the outcome of the interview.

CLOSING THE INTERVIEW

We have emphasised the 'high stakes' nature of the interview. This tends to make it a setting which is especially ripe for you to engage in impression management. At the close of the interview, you are leaving behind a set of impressions for the interviewer to weigh up and then make a decision. While the first four minutes are critical, finishing on a high note is just as important. Think carefully about how you will be judged after leaving the room. Here are some suggestions for you to work on:

■ Do you exude confidence but without coming over as brash and arrogant?
■ Are you polite and considerate but without seeming to be sycophantic or ingratiating?
■ Are you sufficiently nervous to appreciate the occasion but not visibly anxious all the time?
■ Are you open and approachable without being seen as evasive and shifty?

Before the end of the interview, consider how you can reinforce your message so that you actually finish on the high note you are hoping for. You may find these useful:

■ summarise what you see are the key points of the interview;
■ show how far you feel you can match and exceed what's needed to do the job well;
■ if you are still very interested, don't be afraid to reconfirm your keenness;

■ express your thanks and appreciation for the interview;
■ finally, establish when you will be given a decision; the next day, send off your thank you letter.

TIPS TO IMPROVE YOUR INTERVIEW SKILLS

You will find plenty of advice and tips in the many books and articles written about the employment interview. Should you forage through the Internet, there are even more for you to ponder over. If you are experienced and in a senior position, you will have your own 'pet ideas' which you keep working on.

By trying these, you are highly likely to improve your performance.

1. Record several searching face-to-face interviews from serious television programmes. Focus on those involving key public figures who are rigorously cross-examined by highly skilled and perceptive interviewers. Carefully analyse such issues as impression management, body language, structure and length of responses and the use of language and voice. Compare and contrast performances on both sides, picking up tips and techniques which you feel will help you in the employment interview.

2. Before you go to the interview, consider the kind of interaction which is likely to take place between you and the interviewer. For example:

   Are you persuading or negotiating?
   Are you discussing or imparting information?
   Are you receiving information or selling yourself?

   Each type of interaction demands a different strategy on your part. Separate each of these and, for the purposes of your own self-presentation, plan how you would undertake each approach.

3. Try to understand the expectations which others have of you. This is important for two reasons. First because most

people are unaware of other peoples expectations of them. Secondly, in the interview, you will need to seize the opportunity to manage the expectations of the interviewer. What is important is that these expectations of you are positive rather than negative. To discover these, engage in discussions with a wide range of colleagues and friends to obtain feedback. In addition look at your performance appraisal (if to hand) as well as obtaining the views of people in your team, or on your project or assignment. Above all, endeavour to find out what aspects of your performance and personality enhance or impede your effectiveness. Take any criticism constructively since this is the only way you can learn about this important area.

4. It can be very useful to visualise being offered a job and then map out a tentative *action plan* showing what you can offer and how you will go about doing it. In this way, and without being regarded as too presumptuous, you are clearly presenting a set of proposals that will demonstrate how you will add value, while at the same time showing your planning and organising skills.

5. Always present yourself in a positive way, avoiding any phrases which indicate that you are not used to problem solving or that show you are somewhat self-deprecating. For example, rather than saying 'the problem with that was ...', or 'of course that was always a difficult task ...', talk instead about the challenge of devising solutions, the excitement of tackling a thorny issue and coming up with a creative plan of action. Passivity is of little value when trying to portray yourself as an effective problem solver and creative thinker.

8

Other Forms of Selection: What Else Can You Expect to Experience?

INTRODUCTION

In the previous chapter we discussed the significance of the traditional employment interview. In this chapter we will examine other important methods used in selecting managers and professionals. The reason for this is that during your job hunting, as well as in your overall career development, you are highly likely to be assessed by a panoply of selection practices and techniques. These are designed to shed more light on:

- your intellectual capacity and your verbal, numerical and reasoning skills;
- your personality traits and how far these fit the job both now and in the future;
- your value systems and motivation, range and depth of experience, potential for growth;
- your application motives, career preferences, availability, biographical characteristics.

Instead of relying solely on your CV and a single interview, selectors are now looking for far more detail about you, especially if your aspirations are for a senior position. They are not simply interested in your general employability. Instead, they also want to know how good you will be at:

- Fitting into the content of the job – how you will respond to a new team; how you will manage and be managed; how satisfied you will be with rewards and work conditions; how organised you are and what is your preferred management style; how well you perform; how well you adapt to a new job.
- Fitting into the context of the job – how you conduct yourself at work; what are your work values and beliefs; what are your future expectations of the job and the organisation; how far will you show a strong commitment to the prevailing culture.

To obtain such detail, selectors are increasingly using a multi-assessment approach in their constant search for the best person for the job as it stands now and in the future. For example, you may find selectors using such techniques as:

- Assessment/Development centre exercises;
- Psychometric tests of different kinds;
- Biodata, collected by standard application forms or through Biographical Information Blanks (BIBs);
- Graphology (handwriting analysis);
- References, testimonials, letters of recommendation, verbal reports and network referrals.

Behind these different techniques, the results of which are often combined, lies a definite purpose. It is to reduce the risk of making a bad decision, of taking on board the wrong person and then discovering the subsequent high costs of replacement. Therefore, as an applicant you will need to consider how well you are likely to perform when faced with a battery of tests and other assessment procedures. This is not simply because you may already be looking for your next job. Just as important is the prospect that during your current position you may find yourself affected by mergers, take-overs or reorganisation. Your role may be about to change as you come face to face with a re-engineered and refocused business. In such events, employers will view systematic selection as a vital element in their investment decisions.

This makes it increasingly likely you will be tested to see if you fit in, if you can meet performance targets, or if you can take on major responsibilities. Even more important is to find the evidence that you have the adaptability to take on new roles, to learn new tasks and skills and to manage complex projects in an environment of continuous change. The new thinking is about repositioning and responsiveness, about organisational learning, about radical restructuring in order to move from what is done now to what needs to be done in the future. In such situations, selectors are searching for evidence of what you can offer in terms of creativity, innovation, drive and energy. It is these they look for when assessing if people can make a success of jobs and organisations in the early part of the 21st Century.

ASSESSMENT CENTRES

Definitions of assessment centres vary. In essence they are not geographical places but a series of situational exercises, tests, and interviews, usually spread over a period of one to three days, during which you, and several other candidates, will be systematically observed by trained assessors. A variety of assessment instruments are used to measure the different aspects of behaviour revealed by candidates during each exercise. A composite report is given based on pooling the information gathered during the exercises. Assessment centres thus offer an evaluation by different raters or judges of how well you have done over several dimensions or indicators. They are becoming increasingly popular not only for selection but also for training and development, for supervisory purposes and for identifying/predicting future promotability.

Here are a few examples of the kind of indicators or issues which assessors may be looking for when judging how successful you will be in the future:

■ Your interpersonal skills – do you get on with people, are you co-operative and friendly?

- Your oral presentation skills – can you express yourself clearly, use words effectively, summarise?
- Your intellectual skills – are you logical, analytical and able to reach conclusions?
- Your persuasive skills – are you forceful, able to reach agreement and obtain acceptance?
- Your organising and planning skills – are you time sensitive, deadline conscious, goal oriented?
- Your problem solving skills – can you form connections from disparate information and ideas?

Assessment centres not only offer a multiple assessment approach to the selection of candidates. They also try to simulate the actual job in question and then endeavour to achieve a precise fit between the *test environment and the actual work environment*. By giving you the opportunity to display your skills and competencies, you will also provide the assessors with a snapshot of how you are likely to shape up in a real-life situation.

However, for job hunters, assessment centres are of special interest when they are used to decide who is the most suitable applicant competing for a *single* position. If you are invited to attend an assessment centre which focuses on a single job, then you need to be aware what it is designed to do.

- It will monitor, document and then assess your performance during a series of exercises; these will usually be in the form of simulated work situations which measure and evaluate behaviours connected to managerial performance.
- It will be specially designed to draw out from you those behaviours which are seen by assessors as important in successfully performing a particular job, eg problem solving, information processing.
- It will provide you with feedback on how well you have mastered certain essential tasks and how well you have coped in certain situations.

So that you can gain a better insight into this increasingly popular form of selection, particularly where managerial and professional jobs are concerned, let us look more closely at the three major components of an assessment centre. Do bear in mind that this is for selection among competing candidates to identify which one has the most suitable skills for the job. It is not to identify your suitability for training or for promotion in the future.

(1) The assessors

These vary between four and six in number, usually on a ratio of 1:2 assessors to candidates. Depending on the level of the post, they may consist of both internal line managers, with a more senior chairperson, and one or more externals such as occupational psychologists or consultants. An organiser will brief you during the exercises as well as administering the tests and providing support for the assessment panel. Assessors have normally undergone extensive training and practice in both observation and assessment techniques and within controlled settings. The overall objective is for the assessors to reach an informed decision about the suitability of a range of candidates for a specific job. The data collected on your performance will be both quantitative and qualitative. Once all the evidence is collected in respect of your overall performance, this is then relayed in the form of extensive and personal feedback, together with a constructive plan of action to enable you to benefit from the findings. The object is not to pass or fail you, but to establish how far you are better in some roles than others.

(2) The candidates

When used for selection purposes, there are likely to be between five and eight candidates who are assessed together over the specified time period (one to three days). There is likely to be considerable interaction between candidates during some of the formal exercises as well as informally during the breaks.

(3) The exercises

These can last from one to three days. They consist mainly of situational exercises or assessment techniques which are carefully designed to simulate the real world-work activities of the job for which candidates are being considered. Such techniques may include an in-tray exercise, a leaderless group exercise, an interview, a presentation, a case study, as well as several psychometric tests, such as personality, mental ability and aptitude. You may also complete a biographical questionnaire or even interpret a film or video. As a candidate you are likely to be measured along a range of dimensions which can include leadership; energy; tolerance of uncertainty; decision-making; interests; stress resistance; organising and planning; scholastic aptitude. Let us look at two common exercises in more detail to give you a greater 'feel' of what is involved.

The in-tray exercise   You will be presented with a sample of documents which you would expect to appear in a manager's in-tray. These could be internal memoranda, reports, letters, telephone messages, faxes, minutes and copies of e-mail. The samples will vary in importance, urgency and complexity and as such will demand different replies. You will normally work alone within a specified time such as one hour. You will respond to each sample in writing and also complete a 'reason for action' form which you will subsequently expand on to an assessor during a feedback interview. The aim of this exercise is to see how well you can establish the main issues and then prioritise what has to be done, all in a short space of time. In this sense the assessors are trying to compare your behaviour in the exercise with the behaviour in an actual managerial situation.

The case-study   You will be given a specific role within a project and then asked to stand in for a more senior colleague (such as Finance or Operations Director) at a key business meeting. From a file of relevant papers and other briefing material, you will be asked to prepare for the meeting, indicating the main issues involved and the conclusions you have reached. This will normally take one hour and then you will be asked to defend your strategy before an assessor.

What's in it for me?

An assessment centre will endeavour to explore how far you have mastered a range of specified tasks which are seen by the assessors as critical in job performance. By going through the process, you will have the opportunity to show your potential to others across a range of dimensions. Moreover, because you will have a panel of assessors objectively measuring your overall performance, you will be able to take stock, to identify your strengths and weaknesses and to formulate a plan for your future career development.

What can I do to prepare for an assessment centre?

Here are a few ideas for you to consider:

■ Throughout all the exercises, endeavour to act as naturally as possible; don't distort your performance simply to impress the assessors, since they are likely to see through this quite quickly.
■ Don't become demoralised if you perform badly on an exercise; you are unlikely to be good at everything you are asked to undertake and dwelling on it will only affect your subsequent performance.
■ Before the assessment, obtain a clear understanding of the specific requirements of the job for which you are being considered. Think about its responsibilities, its purpose and importance in the organisation, the specific skills and qualities needed and how it will be rated, what behaviours are required and how it may change over time.
■ Put yourself in the assessor's shoes and become a critic of

your own performance; consider ways in which you can improve your presentation skills, interview behaviour, in-tray decision making.

■ Talk to people who have gone through the process, ask for their opinions and how they coped; then construct a check-list of what you need to do to prepare thoroughly for the exercises.

BIODATA – THE JIGSAW OF YOUR LIFE

Your biodata is shorthand for your biographical data. In essence it is a grouping together of different pieces of information about your past. It can be represented as *the jigsaw of your life*. Each piece means something and together they form an overall picture of yourself which you will wish to present in the most favourable way to a potential employer. However, potential employers will be particularly interested in unravelling the picture and examining the individual pieces, often in considerable detail.

■ They will want to know about what you have achieved and under what circumstances; what you have experienced or what you can contribute in the future.

■ They will be concerned about your overall commitment and performance, about your intentions to stay or leave, or about your creativity and ability to fit into an organisation's culture.

In looking for vital clues to all these factors, employers have come to rely especially heavily on biodata. This is because it has been consistently shown over very many years to be one of the most reliable predictors of future job performance. In other words, there is often a strong causal relationship between applicants' previous successes and achievements and whether they will repeat these again in the future. Small wonder therefore that you will find yourself providing a wide variety of information about yourself to potential employers. At interview there may be a distinct focus on your biographical past, especially if you do not have a substantial amount of work exerience behind you. The references or letters of recommendation which are sent on your behalf are also likely to convey biographical data. During your telemarketing you will endeavour to match job requirements with critical aspects of your biodata, showing you are a good fit or match for the job in question.

In addition to these, here are three important ways in which you can market your own biodata and which are likely to be carefully scrutinised by prospective employers:

1. Presenting your CV and any covering letters of application.
2. Completing a standard application form (SAF).
3. Completing a Biographical Information Blank (BIB).

Each of these will give you the opportunity to present yourself as a favourable candidate. However, in order to make a significant impression you will need to carefully assess how you will use each of these forms of biodata exchange in order to enhance your prospects. Previous chapters have focused on your approach to CVs and covering letters as well as your behaviour during different forms of selection interviews. In this section we will look at biodata in more detail. In particular, we will examine links between biodata and identity. Then we will look at different ways of classifying biodata and finally assess how employers use it to judge your suitability as a job applicant.

Biodata and identity

Your biodata inventory contains a wealth of information about yourself and can stretch to literally hundreds of pieces about your past. The ways in which your identity is contoured and developed, in other words who you are and how you behave, is invariably shaped by your biodata. Your birthplace, the background and occupations of your parents, your schooling and pattern of education, your social background and membership of clubs and teams will all have some influence on your beliefs, values, attitudes, career goals and personal aspirations. Your background can both categorise and indeed stigmatise you. Your age may be regarded as a bar to your future progression, or you may be perceived as over-qualified for a job because of your credentials and experience. You may have changed jobs too frequently, or stayed too long in one organisation or sector. Your biodata may show you to have plateaued early or to have failed to develop your early potential. It may also indicate how much further you could progress or what you are really capable of attaining if given the right opportunities and climate. Your ability to identify with the culture and values of an organisation will be an important issue for most selectors, who will be looking for signs of your attachment and commitment both to the job and to individual members of the organisation.

Selectors charged with filling managerial and professional jobs use biodata extensively to address four key issues relating to identity:

- Will the candidate fit into the organisation?
- Will the candidate perform well in the job?
- Will the candidate benefit from further training?
- Will the candidate stay and develop a strong sense of commitment?

In each of these issues, selectors will be endeavouring to establish a link or connection between aspects of your biodata and your future job performance. Whether the link is clear and precise, or vague and ambiguous, is open to debate. As with some other forms of selection, accurately predicting future performance simply by looking at biodata can be very difficult and indeed is open to charges of unfairness and bias. Nevertheless, you will certainly find employers spending considerable time and effort trying to find a causal relationship between aspects of your past and how you will perform in the future. Let us have a look at this in the form of a table.

ITEMS OF YOUR BIODATA	WHAT ARE THESE TRYING TO MEASURE OR IDENTIFY?
Your family background and circumstances	This may predict how well you will achieve in the future
Your record of educational quality of credentials	These may show your future potential and achievement and motivation to succeed
Your hobbies, recreational and leisure interests	These may show your emotional stability and whether you are team centred or a loner; or a joiner and belonger
Your future career plans and goals; where you envisage being in four–five years time	These may indicate how goal centred or realistic you are in developing your career

Employers frequently use biodata information, often in the form of your previous track record, to provide clues to your potential value to their organisation. You may find yourself being closely questioned about your *personal identity* (in terms of your personality and abilities) as well your *social identity* (family background, clubs and associations, group or team membership and how you relate to people from diverse backgrounds and interests).

Classifying biodata

Standard biodata can be represented in terms of particular groupings of information about a person's past. You will have already grouped aspects of your biodata within your CV as well as covering letters. At interview you will try to present biodata in some kind of grouping, to show how each piece in your *life's jigsaw* can be related to your application and what the particular job requires. Here are two examples of classification which you will find valuable in presenting or marketing your own biodata.

Example One
1. *Demographic* – date, place of birth, sex, age, marital status, children, parental history/background
2. *Education* – schools and higher education, qualifications, training, length of schooling
3. *Previous employment and work experience* – number, types of previous jobs, salary progression
4. *Positions of responsibility outside work* – charities, professional institutions, public service, etc
5. *Leisure and social interests* – hobbies, sporting and cultural activities, reading habits
6. *Additional data* – medical, military history, health record, physical characteristics, career goals

Example Two
1. *Background data* – schools, colleges, universities, professional and managerial training, their reputation and standing; your employment history, work experience, family background and circumstances; support during education and training; non-work interests and activities
2. *Commitment data* – your motivation, drive, energy, job involvement, degree of independence, creativity, innovatory skills, levels and types of responsibilities, capacity to lead and manage, ability to identify with corporate goals and culture
3. *Achievement data* – your performance at school, college, university, in your professional development; record of attendance, successes and failures, prizes, awards; sporting, cultural and social achievements; career path and progress; personal development plans

Your biodata will certainly be assessed to see how far you are fitted for a particular role or job, eg

■ Does it show you are bright, stable and achievement oriented with varied operational experience?
■ Does it display you as a conservative and conventional professional on a progressive career path?
■ Does it indicate that you are up-to-date in your field and abreast of new developments?

■ Does it emphasise your adaptability and flexibility and capacity to hit the ground running?

Do not underestimate the power of your biodata – you can use it very effectively to show how you can be a highly desirable candidate. This explains why so much emphasis in job hunting is placed on the design and presentation of your CV and covering letters. At the same time be especially aware how far selectors will rely on signs and trends within your biodata to judge your suitability. Their concerns may relate to such issues as: have you consistently performed well in different settings; have you failed to deliver your earlier promise; have you shown persistence and creativity in problem solving.

Why employers focus on biodata

With increasing competition and the clear need to meet the challenges of turbulent and often unpredictable business environments, employers are continually refining their selection methods. Not only is this to make them more accurate and consistent. It also helps to ensure they are fair and equitable and that they conform to changing legal and other standards. By searching for ways to screen out unsuitable applicants and then select the best candidate for the job or role, selectors are hoping to avoid costly mistakes. They will look especially hard for any signs which would indicate that a candidate may not perform well, or may not stay in the job or may not fit into the prevailing culture. One of the most generally accepted ways of predicting how a person will perform in the future is to carefully analyse how that person has done in the past. However, biodata analysis, like other forms of selection, does not carry a guarantee of success every time. It is often confusing to selectors because it is both objective and subjective, ie it can be classified into hard and usually verifiable data (date of birth, qualifications, periods of unemployment) as well as soft and subjective data (such as extent of experience, values and attitudes) which may be less reliable and capable of exaggeration or misinterpretation.

In order to collect and then analyse biodata, selectors often make use of two techniques, both of which you should aware of if you are hoping to reach the shortlist. These are:

1. Asking you to complete *a standard application form*; this may have been designed to elicit different kinds of biodata to correspond with the requirements of a job, eg physical data like height, weight, eyesight, manual dexterity; special skills like computing or languages; special experience like supply chain management, MRP II, employee relations; particular qualifications like MBA, C. Eng., ACA, Ph.D. Certain items of biodata can be numerically weighted, such as class of degree, type of professional qualification, nature of work experience and level of responsibility. A minimum score may be determined and the higher you are above this, the greater your chances of selection.

2. Requesting you to complete a specially constructed and computerised *Biographical Information Blank (BIB)*, which can consist of 100 or more questions about yourself. The responses you give will be weighted in different ways and then compared with the profile of an ideal or successful job holder. If the information you provide is very similar to the 'successful profile', then you will be judged as highly likely to succeed in the job. If your responses do not correspond closely, you will be rejected because your computer print-out will have shown more failures than successes.

Two tips in presenting your biodata

1. Collect as many items of your personal biodata as possible. Carefully classify them under five major headings of your choice; then use this material in the form of a presentation of some five minutes to answer the question 'why should you select me for this particular job'.

2. Construct a personal biodata inventory, weighting those items which you feel are of special interest to employers. Then assess those items which you feel may receive a negative reaction; where possible, work on these to

improve their attractiveness (eg your professional self-development).

PSYCHOLOGICAL TESTS

Psychological tests are devices which collect samples of behaviour under what are called *standardised conditions*. You are not judged to pass or fail, but your performance is compared against known standards for a similar group of people, such as managers or scientists. These samples are then used to measure different aspects of you as a person, such as your reasoning ability, your aptitudes, or your personality and interests. For example, some tests may show you to be more extrovert than introvert, or more self-assured than apprehensive. Tests can also be used to predict a specific outcome (such as your capacity for further training, or your ability to adapt to a new culture, or your suitability to become a computer programmer). Whatever their purpose, tests are now used extensively in helping organisations to make more informed decisions about whom to select and whom to reject. Recent estimates suggest over 80 per cent of companies now use some form of testing in their selection process. A decade ago, this was calculated to be less than 40 per cent. Therefore an awareness of what tests involve and how they are used will be of considerable benefit to you.

Selectors may use tests not only to determine who is most acceptable but also who is likely to deliver superior performance in the future, thus leading to important productivity gains within an organisation. Such tests, often referred to as psychometric tests, are used to bring a far greater degree of objectivity and fairness into what is often seen by job hunters as the highly subjective and potentially biased business of personnel selection.

When undertaking tests, you will find they differ in form, in their level of difficulty, in their procedures and administration. Some will be valuable in matching your personality to the culture of an organisation, while others will indicate your ability to learn new skills and tasks, or to adapt to rapid change. Again, some tests will be used to see if you have the ideas and creativity to venture into something new and innovative, or to forecast trends and issues, or to help reposition a diverse organisation. Since tests are designed to measure specific attributes, your test scores will often have a numerical value placed against them, such as an I/Q of 129, or a score of 9.2 for anxiety on a 16PF.

Tests gather information in different ways. Some involve a series of questions for which there are alternative answers. Or they may ask you to complete a questionnaire on a self-report basis. Others can ask you to recognise shapes or hidden figures, or interpret pictures, or fit patterns together, or reason with numbers. The stage within the selection process when you actually encounter tests and testing will vary. Some organisations may use tests very early on in order to weed out unsuitable applicants. This is likely when there are large numbers involved, such as graduate trainees for large and popular firms. You may also find you are asked to complete tests after a successful interview, but before being formally offered an appointment. At the other end of the scale, all those short-listed for senior positions may be very carefully tested over two or more days. This often happens when selectors (whether as headhunters or in firms) are looking for a range of specific interests or abilities or personality traits to fit a particular job, eg ability to handle stress or conflict or uncertainty, or design and lead large-scale diverse projects.

WHY TESTS ARE IMPORTANT IN SELECTION

If you are keen to know more detail about your own interests and aptitudes, about your level of reasoning ability, or about your personal values and how far these match certain occupations, then it is highly likely that you will turn to well constructed and soundly researched psychological tests to find some of the answers. You may want to know how adaptable you are in changing your job or career. You may want to discover if you have specific aptitudes to undergo specialised training. Or you may just want confirmation that you are still well suited to, and haven't gone off the boil in, your current role. In all these areas, psychological tests can play an important part in providing you with relevant information. By finding out much more about what you are good at now in comparison with similar people in your field, or by discovering you do have a high level of intelligence and specific interests which will enable you to cope with career change, then such factors are highly likely to boost your self-esteem and confidence.

At the same time, selectors will also be keen to determine how far their demands for specific personality traits or levels of intellectual ability are actually being met by job applicants. For a moment, consider here recent examples of 'essential criteria' taken from advertisements for managers and professionals, eg:

- must possess first class leadership skills combined with a variety of interests inside and outside work;
- strong project management skills alongside strategic vision and commercial realism are essential;
- the ideal candidate will be computer literate, innovative, creative, and have a distinct presence;
- the role calls for competence in persuasive communication, shrewd judgement and analytical ability.

To discover how far candidates can meet these stipulations or desired attributes, selectors will need to have a far richer understanding of individual behaviour than can be gleaned at a subjective interview (in other words, what you see is not necessarily what you get). In order to understand the characteristics underlying a candidate's behaviour they will need to use one of a range of normative tests which measure single personality traits.

Having said that, many candidates still express scepticism, apprehension or even anxiety about taking different psychological tests during their job search. They may have been influenced by others with bad experiences, or just see tests as unfair, prejudiced and favouring only the very bright extrovert.

Again, tests can be criticised because they appear to invade our privacy or try to explore those attitudes or beliefs which we may wish to hide from others. Reputable and experienced test developers are clearly very aware of such issues and therefore take great care to ensure they are only measuring job related attributes.

Clearly, because there is no such thing as a perfect selection system, it follows that tests in themselves cannot guarantee complete accuracy nor can they measure precisely a particular sample of a person's behaviour. However, while tests do not purport to be infallible, research findings consistently show that, in relation to other methods of selection, they are a very distinct improvement, particularly when their reliability and validity receive high ratings.

From your point of view there are several features about them which are important, namely:

- They are regarded as the fairest, most accurate and cost-effective means of obtaining relevant information in order to improve the quality of decisions about the suitability of job candidates.
- They are both objective and subjective in measuring and describing different samples of behaviour collected under standardised conditions. When used correctly, tests provide valuable job-related information for both the selectors and you as a candidate.
- They enable candidates to demonstrate not only their skills, knowledge and potential, but also show their potential for future development, thus aiding their personal career management.
- They indicate that the selection process is taken seriously and methodically: without the benefit of sound, well designed, objective tests, candidates would continue to be selected by highly subjective means such as interviews, references and personal contacts.

EXAMINING DIFFERENT KINDS OF TESTS

As a candidate, you are likely to take a battery of psychological tests, depending on the type of job under consideration and the preferences and experience of the selectors. It is the responsibility of selectors to choose what kinds of tests should be used in order to reach an accurate assessment about your fitness for a particular job, or suitability for training. Because of the variety and complexity of literally hundreds of tests which can be utilised in the area of selection, this section will concentrate on two issues. First, outlining in general terms the main groupings of tests and what they are designed to achieve. Secondly, providing some guidance on how you can approach them in order to perform to the best of your ability.

For selection purposes, psychological tests can be grouped under three main headings, as follows:

Ability tests

These are designed to measure your maximum performance capacity in a particular area. They are concerned with what you know *now*. In other words, how far you have developed your potential and what you have derived from your education, training and overall experience. Many of these kinds of test will measure your problem solving or cognitive skills (known as your underlying general mental abilities). These refer to such things as your verbal comprehension, spatial and logical reasoning, speed of thought, concentration and numerical reasoning. Cognitive tests are essentially tests of achievement, measuring what you have learned or accomplished so far in your life. Other, non-cognitive tests, can be used to measure your manual dexterity or hand-eye co-ordination or your colour vision.

What is important to both candidates and selectors is that a person's general cognitive ability is a very strong predictor of performance in a wide variety of jobs as well as being most significant in their choice of occupation. The reasons for this are that your general cognitive ability equips you to acquire important job knowledge, and such knowledge then leads to improved performance in the job. This general ability is also vital when it comes to mastering complex information, a distinctive feature of many managerial and professional jobs. Increasingly, you will be rated in terms of how you store, select, retrieve, transform and appraise information. Your job may well depend on how quickly you react, how good is your short term memory and how you use these psychological attributes to adapt to changing situations, learn new procedures or tasks, solve problems and recall information critical for job performance.

Examples of general mental ability tests in common use include: *Watson-Glaser Critical Thinking Appraisal; WAIS (Wechsler Adult Intelligence Scale); AH 5; SHL Critical Thinking; Cattell 16PF (B scale); Raven's Progressive Matrices Verbal ability − SHL. VTS; Numerical ability − SHL. NT2, NT4; Spatial ability − SHL ST7*

Personality tests

Selectors frequently turn to personality tests to provide them with unbiased predictions of future performance. In reality these are usually pencil and paper exercises in the form of a questionnaire which can vary in size and detail; some have perhaps 40 questions, others over 500 questions, The more questions asked, the more information it is able to obtain, and hence the more reliable it will usually be. At the same time, longer tests are more expensive to buy, as well as to score and administer. Be aware of very short personality tests which claim to be highly accurate. In terms of style, some questions ask you to answer 'yes' or 'no': or 'like/dislike'; or respond to a rating scale such as 'always ... sometimes ... never'.

Personality questions ask you to give information about what you consider is your typical behaviour in a variety of situations and circumstances. For example, in response to the statement '*I get worked up about things*', you may be forced to make a choice between *frequently, sometimes, rarely*. Another example could be 'I come up with new ideas' – (often, sometimes, seldom). These are known as self-report tests and are based on what you are prepared to divulge about yourself and how accurate you are in rating your own abilities. The responses you make to these and in other tests are scored and then compared and interpreted against a relevant and representative sample.

Selectors are keen to know about your personality traits because these are highly likely to affect your work performance, your productive output and your long-term adjustment to a particular job. Performance indicators such as decisiveness, practical sense, judgement and conscientiousness can all be measured by means of personality tests. Experts in vocational guidance stress that certain personalities fit some jobs better than others. How often do we hear of managers and professionals who in one particular job find enrichment, satisfaction and fulfilment. They then move to another job where they are constrained, dissatisfied and frustrated. In the same way that your personality will be a major issue in why selectors will offer you a job, so you will find that you will also fit better into the 'personality' of one organisation rather than another.

As a general guide, your personality can be grouped under what are called 'the big-five headings':

1. *Your conscientiousness* – including your will to achieve; your dependability and perseverance; how hardworking and organised you are; how far you are careful and responsible.
2. *Your neuroticism* – looking at your concerns, anxieties and phobias; to what extent you are angry, insecure, hyperactive and worried.
3. *Your agreeableness* – how far you are likeable, trusting, compliant, adaptable, flexible and tolerant; your interpersonal skills – are you good natured, sociable, rigid, suspicious?
4. *Your intellect* – how far you are cultured, original, intelligent, artistic, sensitive, broadminded, imaginative, creative.

5. *Your extroversion* – how far you are assertive, expressive, ambitious, active, gregarious, impetuous.

Examples of personality tests in common use include: *16PF; Myers Briggs Type Indicator (MBTI); Minnesota Multiphasic Personality Inventory (MMPI); Eysenck Personality Inventory (EPI); SHL OPQ (several versions)*

Aptitudes and interests

Aptitude tests differ from attainment tests in that they are designed to measure your innate potential, ie how you are likely to perform in the future in terms of acquiring new skills and knowledge. For example, you may sit aptitude tests to determine if you would be suitable for a course of study or to undertake specialist training (eg as a navigator or systems analyst or mechanical engineer). Unlike personality tests, questions set in aptitude tests demand correct answers. Such tests can be very useful to you not only because they draw attention to what your strengths and weaknesses are; they also help in predicting your chances of success when contemplating a major job or career shift. This kind of information will become even more important as managers and professionals continue to develop portfolio careers while spending shorter periods in any one job.

Interests are important in selection because we like to learn things we do well while disliking the things we don't do well. Interest inventories are used to examine your particular preferences within different tasks or activities or roles; for example they can indicate how far you are 'people oriented' or 'task oriented'. They can also alert you to interests which are comparable with occupations you would not normally have considered. In this sense they are most valuable in helping people to make more informed choices, especially when it comes to redundancy counselling or contemplating an important career change.

Examples of Interests Tests in common use include: *SHL Advanced Occupational Interests Inventory; Strong Campbell*

Interest Inventory (SCII) SHL Management Interests Inventory; Holland Vocational Preference Inventory

HOW TESTS CAN HELP YOU

Tests are generally designed to be objective, independent, standardised and non judgmental. They don't purport to replace the employment interview and they don't claim to be infallible in predicting your future performance in a particular job. However, they are helpful in unearthing facts about yourself which may not be possible at interview (for example, your precise I/Q rating, team role preferences, leadership style).

Because of their general neutrality and objectivity, tests also endeavour to enhance fairness and equity into the selection process. Since they operate on a level playing field basis (namely, assessing everyone against the same criteria under uniform conditions), tests go a long way to ensuring that the right person is put into the right job. They can also provide you with the assurance that you are better suited for some things than others. Here are a number of ways in which tests can be of help to you in your job search:

■ They are important in indicating what are your main strengths and abilities, eg high intelligence.

■ They also indicate where you may need to develop your skills, eg improving numerical abilities, increasing experience in particular spheres, coping with stress at work.

■ They give you a clearer picture of how far you are a good fit for a particular job; they enable you to come closer to the job which suits you best by identifying your skills compatibility.

■ They provide another opportunity to present yourself, especially when your interview skills may not be as good as you would wish them to be, or the interview was conducted badly and unfairly.

HOW YOU CAN IMPROVE YOUR SCORES

Because tests vary in quality, cost and appropriateness, it is difficult to give any specific tips or guidance when taking a particular test. Indeed, for the vast majority of tests, you will find very stringent conditions attaching to their purchase, distribution and use by registered and qualified testers. For more general information about psychological tests, you will find *The Mental Measurements Yearbook (Buros)* of considerable value. This provides details and critical reviews of the majority of tests available, including their strengths and weaknesses. Other useful reference works, often to be found in large public libraries or larger university libraries, include *Test Critiques; Tests in Print; Testing Adults*. There are also several general books such as *How to Pass Selection Tests; How to Pass Graduate Recruitment Tests; Test Your Own Aptitude. The Handbook of Psychological Testing* by Paul Kline is highly informative.

Here are several general guidelines which you can follow:

- Don't be put off by the thought of doing tests; you will invariably find them fun and informative.
- Turn up in plenty of time, feeling relaxed, refreshed, motivated and keen to do your best.
- Approach them in a constructive and confident way; the more you try, the more you will achieve.
- Learn to work quickly and accurately during the test; nearly all have time limits.
- Try to become familiar with the kind of questions you are likely to be asked; if possible, obtain practice tests but bear in mind that reputable tests are very carefully controlled and not generally available.
- Read all instructions very carefully and follow the rubric exactly. If you are uncertain of some answers and time permits, check them again. If you decide to guess, make sure you are not penalised.
- Don't panic; look at the examples and think carefully, especially in numerical and intelligence tests.

- Don't waste time dwelling on difficult questions but push on and return to these later on.
- Whatever you do, do not lie or fake your answers since many tests have lie detectors within them. If discovered, you will be seen as untrustworthy and will soon face rejection.
- Practise solving puzzles, numerical, mechanical and other tests often seen in newspapers and magazines; search in large newsagents or good book shops for examples such as *Logical Challenge Expert*.

WHAT QUESTIONS SHOULD YOU BE ASKING ABOUT TESTS?

Because psychological testing has become a rather emotive and controversial issue over the last decade, it could be reassuring to ask some important questions relating to the tests that you may be asked to complete. Clearly, not all tests are equal and some are distinctly better than others. Those which have been subjected to many years of research, validation and extensive evaluation are going to be far more reliable and valid than those which have not gone through this rigorous process. Asking questions is not so that you can appear clever and smart. Rather is it to give you a general feeling of confidence in the procedures and above all an assurance that what you are purportedly being tested for (eg leadership skills, team building skills) is actually measurable by the tests.

Here are a few suggestions for you to consider:

- Is the organisation registered and trained in the use of well established, standardised tests?
- What kinds of tests will be used; are they regularly employed to predict performance or behaviour?
- Have the tests been registered with the British Psychological Society?
- Why have particular tests been chosen and are they up-to-date, culturally fair and objective?

- What will the tests involve and how long are they likely to take to complete?
- What results will be relayed to you as a candidate and in what form (scores, verbal, written report)?
- Is the conduct of the tests undertaken by trained and experienced administrators?
- Will the interpretation of the test results be undertaken by an experienced Chartered Psychologist?
- Will the results be confidential and who will have access to them now and in the future?
- Will the tests actually measure the attributes you are looking for, and are these job-related?
- Do the test developers provide statistical evidence to demonstrate the test is reliable and valid?
- To what extent will the test results affect the final decision?

CONCLUSION

As we approach the millennium, the selection of managers and professionals is changing significantly. Not only is the operating environment very different from a decade ago, but in many cases far more care is being taken to quantify the benefits which flow from improved selection. Poor decisions may not be easily reversed due to prevailing legislation. Taking the wrong person on board can soon bring loss of business, impair personal relationships, upset teams and lead to bad publicity through industrial tribunals. As a result, selectors are much keener to statistically measure individual performance during selection; hence the emphasis on psychometric testing and assessment centre exercises.

As a job hunter, your interest in the selection process will be motivated by two key issues. First, you will want to discover how far an organisation makes itself attractive to you as an applicant, eg:

- Is it presenting itself in a positive and attractive way, being open and making you feel welcome?

- Does it go out of its way to discover your needs and career aspirations?
- Are decisions about your application reached fairly and equitably; are you treated courteously?
- Does it provide the structure, support mechanisms, culture and prospects to enable you to prosper and develop your potential?

Secondly, you will want to know which selection methods you are likely to encounter to ensure the job is right for you and you are right for the job. This chapter, along with the previous one on employment interviews, has set out to do this by looking at several alternative ways of predicting future job performance among competing candidates. In the years ahead you will find employers increasingly turning to multi-assessment ways of selecting the best candidates from those available. With evidence that high quality candidates will become both scarcer and more highly sought after, selectors will be even more concerned 'to get it right first time'. While standard and well-developed ability tests would appear to have considerable advantages over the other methods we have explored, it does not seem feasible that these will become the sole method of selecting managers and professionals. Interviews, the use of biographical information and assessment centres, even references and referrals, will still continue to play their parts. However, these will be subjected to continual refinement and development in order to reach what can be called a more informed and holistic evaluation of job applicants.

In your future job hunting, it will become even more important for you to look at this multi-assessment approach (ie interviews, tests, biodata, assessment centres) against the backcloth of rapid and often unpredictable changes in the business environment. Consider here the impact of globalisation, of technological developments, increasing competition and the constant restructuring of operations as identified in earlier chapters. These will not only alter the meaning and purpose of work. They will also create far reaching changes in performance appraisal, in job responsibilities, in team organisation, in support technology and multi-tasking environments. A crucial question which you will need to address in the light of these 'emerging issues' will be *'how are these likely to affect my future employability?'* This is what we will focus on in the next and final chapter.

Part Four:

Securing Your Future Employability

9

Your Future Employability: How to Stay Competitive in the Job Market

INTRODUCTION

In this last chapter we emphasise the importance of your future employability. We explore this against a backcloth of current concerns about job security and the changing nature of the *psychological contract*. Awareness of these issues will enable you to put in place the final pieces of the jigsaw of your job hunting strategy. Our aim is twofold. First, we will examine the background to employability, showing *why* managers and professionals should focus their efforts on being employable rather than being employed. Secondly, we will review some of the latest trends in the labour market and explore *how* you can build personal strategies to maintain your employability in the future.

Employability, as opposed to employment, has become a fashionable term. Since the end of the 1980s, on both sides of the Atlantic, it has become an accepted part of new management thinking both at governmental and corporate levels. The Canadian government has dramatically redirected its unemployment insurance policy from passive support and dependence to active support and independence. Similar switches in policy at federal and state level have occurred in the USA under the Clinton administration. Within the UK, government policy has clearly shifted towards employability. There is much greater emphasis on investing in people, encouraging job creation and lowering dependency on unemployment benefits. Programmes that enhance employee skills and business performance are more in line with an emerging, flexible labour market. Consider here initiatives such as the job seekers allowance, the Private Finance Initiative (PFI), enhanced provision of education and training, and more help with job search skills for the long term unemployed. All these different approaches are trying to build verbal, numerical, interpersonal and team-work skills as well as cognitive and lifelong learning skills. The overall emphasis is one of fostering job creation within a continually changing labour market, in which individuals will need to show flexibility and also acquire these skills to sustain their employability.

At the corporate level, we see the changing structures, shapes and boundaries of business and public sector organisations transforming the work patterns of managers and professionals. Earlier we mentioned such things as core and peripheral workers, interim managers, annualised hours, flexitime, outsourcing and increasing self-employment. In addition, we find the very nature of the employment contract between employer and employee altering. The future permanence of many jobs could be threatened as conditions of employment change, For the individual, fears and anxieties arise about long-term prospects. A gap begins to emerge between what you would ideally like to happen to your job in the long term and what is actually occurring around it.

In essence, what these important changes have caused is a major collision. This is between the ideal of job-tenure and security and the reality of job-insecurity resulting from downsizing, layoffs and restructuring. Expectations of long-term employment security (ie institutionally dependent careers, especially within large corporations in Canada, USA, UK and Japan as examples) were prevalent in the period 1950–1980. These are now giving way to a new form, termed *employability security*. This is where your security no longer resides in a particular organisation or job. Instead it is in your ability to develop a range of academic and professional skills, as well as workplace expertise, so that you can progress in your job and career.

We have already seen that organisations often take quite drastic actions to safeguard their own survival and long term security. As a result, individuals are now examining the very bases and assumptions on which their future job security rests. In the next decade, moving from full-time dependent employee to independent self-directed employment will mean large numbers of managers and professionals coming to terms with their future employability. They are far less likely to rely on a single career in the same organisation over a working lifetime. Instead, as the rules of the game change, many will have to reassess their attitudes, especially if they are over forty. All these issues demonstrate just how the nature of work is changing as we move towards *a more flexible post-industrial economy*.

Where do you go from here? Your aim will be to reposition yourself so that:

- you actively maintain up-to-date skills and knowledge in your current position;
- you continually build up your experience and credentials to fit yourself for jobs in the future.

WHAT IS MEANT BY EMPLOYABILITY?

Let us look at several different approaches to the idea. This will build up a clearer picture of what it means and what it involves.

- 'employability is essentially a new social and psychological contract within the changing workplace which replaces the old idea of a job for life and its attendant security'
- 'employability is based on the idea that a person's future security in the labour market is related to competency and not company'

■ 'employability is about becoming more self-reliant in the new employment relationship in which both sides become less symbiotic and less dependent'

■ 'employability relates to people taking control of their careers and their ability to adapt to changes in the labour market throughout their working life'

■ 'employability is the mixture of skills and experience which you try to sell in the labour market'

What these different interpretations show is that employability is a set of responses to a very changed situation. It is about developing a range of effective personal strategies to face the undeniable fact that jobs previously considered to be secure have come under threat and will continue to do so. For some managers and professionals, stable, long-term jobs will still be available. In some sectors, the average job duration may only fall gradually over the next decade, as it has done over the last two decades.

In the USA for example, figures released by the Department of Labor indicate that, for men, job tenure (ie average time spent in current job) was 5.7 years in 1963, 4.6 years in 1973 and 5.1 years in 1991. During this period, job tenure for women rose from 3.0 to 3.8 years. In the UK, according to research findings from the LSE, average job tenure for men was 7.9 years in 1975 and 6.4 years in 1993. Women's jobs, on the other hand, were shown to last 10 per cent longer in 1995 than in 1975.

Despite these figures, what is important is that job tenure in many sectors is set to fall quite significantly in the next five years. Surveys over the last few years consistently report that feelings of job insecurity have become a relatively permanent state for large numbers of employees at all levels. Much of this stems from increasing organisational transformation, the fall out from mergers, acquisitions, joint-ventures, competition, downsizing and severe cost cutting. These changes are unlikely to go away.

Therefore, trust in one's employer, confidence in one's competence and skill, assurance that the future will be bright are all issues that you will need to assess. As a job hunter, the links between your employability and security are especially significant. This is because insecurity affects vital issues such as your job satisfaction and organisational commitment, your performance outcomes and how you handle stress. As so many redundant managers can testify, experiencing insecurity where once there was relative security not only raises your anxiety level, it also creates strong feelings of ambiguity and powerlessness as well as your loss of identity and confidence.

It would seem then that a curious and perplexing situation has now arisen in the modern workplace. On the one hand, we have employers striving to compete effectively in a rapidly changing global marketplace. To do this they have to attract, retain, motivate and utilise the most talented people they can muster. On the other, employees find the climate and psychological contract changing. Around them there is less security, less predictability and less certainty. To crown all this, there is more stress, more emphasis on individual performance and contribution and more hours put into the job.

REVIEWING THE OLD PSYCHOLOGICAL CONTRACT

The idea of a *job for life* has about it a feeling of some golden age long since gone. In many respects the idea has been mythical, and has only been part of the work culture during the second half of this century. Indeed, since the late 1940s large employers on both sides of the Atlantic were largely expected to provide jobs, and even endeavour to guarantee a range of benefits as well as various forms of upward mobility. The deal appeared simple. Long-term employment (the jobs for life syndrome) was seen as a way of building a highly committed, highly productive workforce. High levels of job security boosted individual job performance. Thus loyal, conscientious employees, especially those in managerial and professional groups who had built up over a decade of service, could expect to end their careers with the organisation. This applied especially within large conglomerates in the UK that, from the late 1940s up to the early 1970s, were increasingly built on bureaucratic and hierarchical principles. From graduate trainee, you could make steady progress through the ranks of junior and middle management up to senior management. The environment of job security, coupled with entitled benefits and the expectation of advancement was strongly pervasive. Built into this longevity covenant was a dependency relationship, rather like a parent to a child. It was certainly one in which middle managers in particular tended to flourish as they were offered promotion prospects, internal training and long term benefits. Loyalty, attachment and commitment were much in evidence. The culture was paternalistic, in which status, identity and emotional bonding were all part of what is known as the *transactional contract*.

However, and perhaps with the benefit of hindsight, shrewd observers felt that in many large firms this was a disaster waiting to happen. Two faulty assumptions on the part of large corporate employers could no longer be sustained:

1. their sales growth, size and stability would continue to protect them against limited competition;
2. economic growth would continue with little reason to change traditional bureaucratic structures, market strategy, operating technology or trading relationships.

Nevertheless, a sea-change was already in motion. By the end of the 1980s the emphasis in maintaining competitive advantage had moved from size, economies of scale and market share to speed and flexibility in meeting customers' demands for higher quality and lower prices. The sheer size of many corporate enterprises became a considerable handicap in adapting to these new market conditions. Drastic action to cut costs through headcount reduction thus became the norm. This led in turn to a fundamental reassessment of the old *transactional contract*. Those who traditionally claimed property rights to their jobs were to experience a rude shock. This was no longer feasible.

FORGING THE NEW RELATIONAL CONTRACT

Over the last 15 years the environment for jobs and careers has altered, often quite dramatically. Instead of top-down, bureaucratically controlled hierarchies (essentially mechanistic) we are seeing the rapid growth of flat network structures, joint ventures, open communications, permeable boundaries and project-led teamwork in what are known as organic enterprises. In business terms, fat is out and flat is in. Here are a few examples of such changes chosen from literally dozens of case studies of corporate reshaping and labour market turbulence.

Pressures to change the organisation	Resulting reactions
Adjusting to intense global competition	→ Streamline operations, cut labour costs
Increased pace of acquisitions and mergers	→ Slim down corporate HQ and support functions
Meeting the challenge of deregulation	→ Make business strategies more focused
Enhancing, unlocking shareholder value	→ Unbundle, restructure, downsize
Facing up to a new business environment	→ Focus on performance, creativity, flexibility
Improving and speeding up communications	→ Delayer, reduce bureaucracy, re-engineer
Information sharing and faster learning	→ Build project-led teams, competencies

Arising from all this, figures show that in the USA alone, some 43 million jobs have been lost overall since 1979. Of these, some 16 million white collar jobs were lost in the period 1989–92. At the same time, since 1979 there has been a net increase of some 27 million jobs, demonstrating considerable turbulence and what is termed 'churn' in the US labour market. Figures for the UK are less specific but churn and turbulence has been on a similar scale. All these have clearly affected our attitude to security at work. The advocates of downsizing point to the need to reduce costs in order to build a viable future. Those laid-off point to the considerable hardship, stress and distrust generated within communities and work environments.

A summary contrasting both transactional and collaborative approaches is given below.

The Old Dependency Relationship	The New Collaborative Relationship
Based on Company rather than competence	Based on individual competency/ performance
Long-term employment tenure prospects	You are in the job only while it lasts
Hard work and controls in exchange for security	You are in charge of own development and career
Paternalistic culture encouraging dependence	Employability is our own responsibility
Work is company specific and inward focused	Employer provides rewards, training, contracts
Strong obligation to employees; caring culture	Employee learning and development plans
Contract based on loyalty, duty, obligation	Contract based on commitment and contribution
Functional specialisation, command and control	Ready transfer of skills to new tasks and jobs

EMPLOYEES, EMPLOYERS AND THE NEW EMPLOYABILITY

We have already discussed several factors that tend to drive job loss in some industries. We can summarise these as technological developments, competitive pressures, investor demands for increased profits, contracting out of work, exchange rate movements, mergers and streamlining. What these do is to create uncertainty and even greater job insecurity, On the other hand such changes also bring about the rise of new jobs and new challenges and opportunities. Some of today's global computer corporations were minions less than a decade ago. To build a new form of security, serious attempts at several levels are now being made to create a greater degree of trust between employee-employer while endeavouring to raise skill levels to meet the needs of the changing workplace. One important aspect, especially in large corporate enterprises, is to move the psychological relationship from being largely *dependent* to being essentially *collaborative*. *As a job hunter, the new security for you is to be seen as employable, not simply employed*. Let us look at this in a little more detail to see what it involves and implies for both sides in this new collaborative partnership.

The employee

Over the next ten years an increasing number of managers and professionals will see their identity linked to the market place rather than a single firm or employer. For you as a job hunter, this is likely to mean:

■ taking more responsibility for your own career and self-development; for younger managers and professionals this will become a necessary and accepted part of their daily work;

■ looking after number one, acting in your own best interests, being far less reliant on an employer as you come to own your own employability;

■ broadening your range of skills to enhance your individual value and security as an independent contractor in the competitive market place; in other words, your self-sufficiency will become a critical component of your employability.

If you are in a high performance workplace, the emphasis will be on developing your technical and managerial knowledge, on continuous learning, on team building and project management. Above all it will be to do with demonstrating your high marketability when the time comes to move on. Setting and exceeding current targets and expectations, finding your own customers, building up your own network and strategic alliances will be an essential part of your new employability. Yet these are developments that are strangely unfamiliar and even disturbing for many managers and professionals. In many ways they are far less prepared than they should be. What is changing is not only the status of the relationship with an employer, but also the emergence of what is known as the *contingency workforce*. This is where you are hired and fired according to fluctuations in the market. This new realism contains within it a new harshness in which past performance and contribution will not be an automatic guarantee of your future job security. Several commentators regard this as a leap in the dark for managers and professionals unaccustomed to undertaking a radical audit of their employability. An interesting piece of recent research shows that only a small proportion of managerial and professional groups devote more than 20 hours of their time in any one job to personal career planning. These developments will doubtless bring a new urgency to accumulate and refine your job search skills in the future. This is not only to help you find jobs that match your current skills and experience. It applies also to jobs you will go for in the future, which are likely to demand very different competencies.

The employer

In future a large majority of employers are unlikely to replace the old certainties and securities with something similar that will then reduce the detrimental effects of insecurity and job loss. In a high proportion of workplaces in the UK, it will be anachronistic and unrealistic to offer job security on the old model. Instead, the nature of the new psychological contract will be based on a set of different assumptions about jobs and the nature of work. Many jobs will be on a temporary, perhaps fixed contract basis, with renewability dependent on both organisational and individual performances. You will find far less loyalty and far fewer entitled benefits. Your advancement will be based on a snake and ladder's scenario, not on a stable corporate climbing frame. Employers will be expected to own the jobs they offer but at the same time give people opportunities to develop new competencies and skills. They in turn can transfer these to another workplace when the job or contract ends. In addition the employer will be expected to provide a challenging, motivating and learning environment in which people grow and develop but which they can nevertheless leave if other opportunities emerge. The motto over the entrance door to the office or factory is more likely to read *'We don't get married here, we just remain good friends'*.

One key issue will be the training and development opportunities offered to the new *contract knowledge workers*. In some cases employers, to attract and retain key staff, will invest substantially in training programmes. Instead of seeing this as training people to *leave* your organisation, this will be increasingly perceived as training people to *stay*. This will then accentuate their employability. The curious paradox is that employers will be able to make it easier for people to stay by providing a more supportive and challenging job environment. Individuals on the other hand will become more secure in the knowledge that they are eminently employable. Where training is not fully supplied by employers, then the responsibility will fall partly on government agencies and partly on yourself to enhance your credentials and certification. This will involve building a different form of trust, a different sense of purpose and a less threatening work environment in order to motivate and retain key knowledge workers. All this may sound good in theory, but there are substantial doubts over how far it can be achieved without a considerable degree of conflict, angst and personal readjustment.

EMPLOYABILITY SKILLS AND SURVIVAL TACTICS IN THE CHANGING WORKPLACE

When we examine the various attempts now being made to

forge a new form of psychological contract between employer and employee, we find they are trying to do two things:

1. They are seeking to reduce the detrimental effects of job loss, such as loss of self-esteem and identity.
2. They are trying to build a set of work-based and non-work based support mechanisms to assist people to move jobs and develop careers in a world of work which is changing, uncertain and unpredictable. Instead of yearning for a return to high levels of security and job continuity, managers and professionals will need to adjust to a workplace rapidly moving away from this former 'ideal state'.

If you are to face this new realism, the key question will be – *what can I do to prepare for this new employability?*

Here we suggest two approaches, which you will need to integrate. The first one is directed towards developing yourself as a *business*. The second one is concerned with positioning yourself as a *knowledge worker*.

YOU AS A BUSINESS

1. Start off by thinking of yourself as a business with different yet interdependent functions such as marketing, finance, R&D, customer service, publicity etc. Your aim is to offer a product or service to customers. Conduct a realistic audit on how good you are in these different functions by comparing them to a business which is successful. Benchmark yourself against set criteria.
2. Next, ask yourself if you are in the right business. Examine the potential for growth in the next five years, assess if current prospects could be affected by advancing technologies or competitors. Consider how far you should be diversifying if you are not correctly positioned in the market.
3. Then think of yourself as a marketing operation. Research

and evaluate your target market. Clearly define your product or service, spelling out your area of expertise and unique selling points. Show how you can add value in terms of your performance. Determine why customers should purchase your services and what you need to do to ensure your *added value* continues to attract customers. Keep your head up to focus on the *context* of what is going on around you. At the same time do not neglect to keep your head down to focus on the *content* of your job and your own performance within it.

4. Continually assess your performance; whether it really is outstanding or simply run of the mill. Establish benchmarks which will distinguish you as innovative and creative and not just another manager (JAM). Differentiate yourself by continually delivering quality and customer satisfaction. Determine how far you have met and exceeded set targets and what objectives still elude you.

5. Finally, set in place a contingency plan that involves changing direction. Jobs and customers don't last for ever so don't make yourself too comfortable. Watch for danger signs of decline such as narrowing margins and loss of market share. Keep an eye on mergers and markets, competitor activity, policy shifts, changes in key personnel. Keep your CV and networking activities up to date. *Above all, reassess your situation* every six months; if you leave it a year it could be too late, especially in chaotic, turbulent environments. If you do lose your job, try to ensure you have sufficient financial resources to survive a period of redundancy.

YOU AS A KNOWLEDGE WORKER

As a manager or professional, you will increasingly find yourself part of a rapidly expanding knowledge network over the next few years. Already, over 50 per cent of UK gross domestic product is knowledge-based and set to grow significantly. Thomas A. Stewart in his recent book *Intellectual Capital; The New Wealth of Nations*, emphasises that 'knowledge has become the most important factor in economic life'. Knowledge workers, through their intellectual capital, will increasingly act as drivers of productivity and economic growth. Following on this, greater effort will be given in the future to measuring what seem to be intangibles, such as our knowledge stocks, knowledge creation and knowledge distribution. Therefore, correctly positioning yourself as a knowledge worker will be an integral part of your employability. At the same time be aware that change can bring both threats and opportunities and it is your job as a knowledge worker to be able to react positively to these in the future.

Here are four suggestions for your consideration:

1. Establish a personal development plan that you should endeavour to link into your current organisation's corporate plan. Matching your goals with that of your employers will enable you to enhance your support networks and build up alliances; these in turn will give you a greater insight into the politics of your organisation, an issue you should not ignore.

2. Pay careful attention to your continuous professional development (CPD). Not only does this involve keeping your current skills up to date; you should be looking to add new ones. Some will improve your personal productivity such as advanced computing, finance or marketing. Others will build your personal confidence and enhance your career prospects. Your professional institute or association could be a valuable source for guidance and ideas.

3. Show a strong commitment to lifelong learning by adding relevant credentials, obtaining certification, undertaking specialised training (all of which should be transferable). Since knowledge obsolescence soon sets in, read widely, attend courses and conferences, and keep abreast of trends and issues in your sector and specialist area.

4. Rigorously analyse your current job to see what

competencies are needed to perform more effectively in the future. Consider how far your current performance indicators, gleaned from 360° feedback, accurately predict your future performance. Look for danger signs. You could be seen as hostile, arrogant, selfish, sloppy. You may fail to meet deadlines, targets or expectations. If so, then you will need to take positive action to remedy these.

CONCERNS FOR THE FUTURE

Like many management fads and fashions, this transactional contract may appear to be a sensible and realistic approach to the major changes affecting the labour market both now and in the future. However, it does have within it a number of paradoxes and inconsistencies which are likely to cause considerable concern especially to those who do not have sound contingency plans. Here are four of these:

1. Taken at face value, you could view the new contract as relieving employers of their previous responsibility of providing a degree of stability and security in their employment relationship. In other words, the transition from dependency to independence will mean that the workplace is likely to be far less trustworthy. This could then lead to far less commitment, loyalty, creativity and productivity.
2. On the other side of the coin of employability could be expendability. If jobs are more transitory, managers and professionals could become more vulnerable in the face of market changes. This in turn will involve them in reassessing and balancing their long term liabilities, eg pension, investment, insurance, mortgage and family responsibilities, in the light of short term job tenure and likely interruptions to income flow.
3. You could argue all this is a convenient way of hiding the real problem. Namely, what can be done to offset the

effects of job loss when people lose their self-esteem, identity and productivity.

4.   Taken at face value, it assumes employees who are bonded, obligated and fettered can somehow shake off the chains of their work environment. They then substitute this for the rather illusory freedom of being a free agent in a rapidly changing labour market. However, for many this transition will be a painful and difficult learning exercise. It will have its pitfalls and failures. Many doubt how far the new transactional contract is sustainable in the long term. If it turns out to be remote, arms-length, temporary and ever-shifting, then your status and identity as well as your emotional bonds with your employer will certainly need a rethink.

TAKING ACTION, REMAINING POSITIVE

Throughout this book we have urged you to approach your job hunting in a proactive and creative way. We have stressed that this important activity should be re-assessed against a backcloth of changes in careers, organisations and the nature of work. In so doing, we have provided you with a set of tools, techniques and tips to help you overcome the various hurdles you are likely to encounter. We have examined tools such as your CV, your covering letters and your personal portfolio. We have explored techniques such as telemarketing, networking and impression management. We have also included a wide range of tips on such issues as electronic job searching, non-verbal behaviour, going for an interview, and managing your career and future development. We have also emphasised that to remain employable, you will have to invest in yourself. This means taking charge of your career and being constantly aware that this will take place in fast changing and often chaotic environments. We have indicated that safe, predictable, secure work is no longer a viable option for the vast majority of managers and professionals. Instead, the new workplace, now and in the future, will be increasingly dominated by knowledge driven organisations. These will demand higher levels of flexibility and adaptability among managers and professionals, whose skills will need to be up-to-date and transferable. All in all, this will mean looking at your job hunting in a different light. It offers excitement and indeed challenge because there will always be something new to learn. This could involve you keeping up with developments in electronic job search, or researching for a career change, or taking on interim roles which demand innovation and creativity. We very much hope that this book has enabled you to look anew at job search; its clear message is one of inspiration, encouragement and hope for the future.

Where then do you go from here? What we are encouraging you to do now is twofold:

First, adopt an action perspective about your job hunting. To cope with uncertainty, take on board our advice about continually developing your network of contacts, keeping abreast of what's happening in the job market, appraising what you have to offer, and investing in yourself through additional credentials and relevant training. Herein lies your future employability.

Secondly, whether you are in work or coping with redundancy, remain focused, optimistic and positive. Job hunting, as we have attempted to show, is not some magic formula, but a set of skills and techniques which can be studied and improved upon. Nevertheless, the rules of the game are changing. Do not look upon it as an occasional exercise, but as a continual learning process. This will help you to maintain your confidence, enthusiasm and commitment and ultimately ensure your successful performance on the shortlist.

Further Reading

Belbin, R. Meredith (1997) *Changing The Way We Work*, Butterworth-Heinemann, Oxford.

Belbin, R. Meredith (1996) *The Coming Shape Of Organisation*, Butterworth-Heinemann, Oxford.

Bolles, Richard Nelson (published annually) *What Colour Is Your Parachute*, Ten Speed Press, Berkeley.

Bridges, William (1995) *Jobshift – How to Prosper In A Workplace Without Jobs*, Nicholas Brealey, London.

Clark, Frances, A. (1992) *Total Career Management*, McGraw Hill Book Company, Maidenhead.

Duncan, J. and Oates, D. (1997) *Career Paths For The 21st Century*, Century, London.

Golzen, Godfrey and Garner, Andrew (1990) *Smart Moves*, Basil Blackwell, Oxford.

Hammer, C. and Champy, J. (1994) *Re-engineering The Corporation*, Harper Business, New York.

Handy, Charles (1984) *The Future Of Work – Making Sense Of The Future*, Arrow Books, London.

Handy, Charles (1995) *The Empty Raincoat – Making Sense Of The Future*, Arrow Books, London.

Handy, Charles (1997) *Beyond Certainty – The Changing World of Organisations*, Arrow Business, London.

Herriot, Peter and Pemberton, Carole (1995) *Competitive Advantage Through Diversity*, Sage, London.

Herriot, Peter (1992) *The Career Management Challenge*, Sage, London.

Johnson, Mike (1996) *The Aspiring Manager's Survival Guide*, Butterworth-Heinemann, Oxford.

Kanter, Rosabeth M. (1992) *When Giants Learn To Dance*, Routledge, London.

Mabey, Christopher and Iles, Paul (1996) *Managing Learning*, International Thomson Business Press, London.

Mayo, Andrew (1991) *Managing Careers – Strategies for Organisations*, IPM, London.

Nicholson, N. and West, M. (1989) *Managerial Job Change*, Cambridge University Press, Cambridge.

Probst, Gilbert and Büchel, Bettina (1997) *Organisational Learning*, Prentice Hall, Hemel Hempstead.

Prusak, Laurence (ed) (1997) *Knowledge in Organisations*, Butterworth Heinemann, Oxford.

Rosenfield, Paul *et al* (1995) *Impression Management In Organisations*, Routledge, London.

Sarch, Yvonne (1991) *How To Be Headhunted*, Arrow Business, London.

Schein, Edgar H. (1994) *Career Survival – Jobs And Role Planning*, Jossey Bass, San Francisco.

Starkey, Ken (1996) *How Organisations Learn*, International Thomson Business Press, London.

Stewart, Thomas S. (1997) *Intellectual Capital – The New Wealth Of Nations*, Nicholas Brealey, London.

Index

234 ■ FROM CV TO SHORTLIST